BRIDGE
BASICS

Other Bridge Materials by Ron Klinger

Published by Modern Bridge Publications

The Modern Losing Trick Count • Bridge for Children
The Power System • Bridge Made Easy
Bridge in Easy Stages • Cue Bidding to Slams
Guide to Better Bridge • Guide to Better Duplicate
Guide to Better Card Play
(Winner of 1991 American Bridge Teachers' Bridge Book of the Year Award)
Practical Slam Bidding • The Bridge Player Who Laughed
Bid Better, Much Better • 5-Card Major Stayman
Bridge Master Class Bridge CD
Flippers on Standard Bridge, The Acol System • Pamphlets on Doubles, Negatives
Doubles, Transfers Over 1NT, 10 Great Conventions, 12 More Great Conventions,
Opening Leads, 1NT: 2♣ Extended Stayman, Roman Key Card Blackwood, Multi-2s,
Cue-Bidding to Slams, Benjamin Twos, Competitive Bidding

Published by Victor Gollancz, Orion,
Cassell & Co, Weidenfeld, and Nicolson (all UK)

Basic Bridge: The Guide to Good Acol Bidding and Play
Right Through the Pack Again (Winner 2009 IBPA Book of the Year)
Power Acol • Improve Your Declarer Play at No-Trumps
Acol Bridge Made Easy • Improve Your Opening Leads
Improve Your Bridge Memory • Better Bridge with a Better Memory
Guide to Better Acol Bridge • Cue Bidding to Slams
Bridge Conventions, Defenses & Countermeasures
100 Winning Bridge Tips • 50 More Winning Bridge Tips
100 Winning Duplicate Tips • Playing to Win at Bridge
Master Class • Ron Klinger Answers Your Bridge Queries
The Power of Shape • When to Bid, When to Pass • To Win at Bridge
Flippers on the Law of Total Tricks, Basic Acol, Opening Leads
20 Great Conventions Flipper • Modern Losing Trick Count Flipper
Duplicate Bridge Flipper • Memory Aids & Useful Rules Flipper

with David Bird: Kosher Bridge • Kosher Bridge 2
The Rabbi's Magic Trick: More Kosher Bridge
with Andrew Kambites: Bridge Conventions for You
Card Play Made Easy 1: Safety Plays and Endplays
Card Play Made Easy 2: Know Your Suit Combinations
Card Play Made Easy 3: Trump Management
Card Play Made Easy 4: Timing and Communication
Understanding the Contested Auction
Understanding the Uncontested Auction
Understanding Duplicate Pairs
Understanding Slam Bidding
with Hugh Kelsey: New Instant Guide to Bridge
with Mike Lawrence: Opening Leads • Opening Leads Flipper
with Derek Rimington: Improve Your Bidding and Play

BRIDGE BASICS

A Beginner's Guide
6th Edition

Ron Klinger

Australian Bridge Federation Grand Master
A.B.F. record Master Point winner 1975–1980
World Bridge Federation International Master
Winner of State and National Championships 1969–2010
Represented Australia in winning 1970 Far East Championships
Winner Far East Open Pairs Championship 1985 and 1987
Winner 1993 South Pacific Zone Teams Championship
Winner 2006 Pacific Asia Seniors Teams Championship
Represented Australia in World Championships in
1976, 1978, 1980, 1984, 1986, 1988, 1989, 1993, 2000,
2003, 2004, 2005, 2006, 2007, 2008, 2009, 2010

Skyhorse Publishing

To Suzie

Skyhorse Publishing books may be purchased in bulk at special discounts for sales promotion, corporate gifts, fund-raising, or educational purposes. Special editions can also be created to specifications. For details, contact the Special Sales Department, Skyhorse Publishing, 307 West 36th Street, 11th Floor, New York, NY 10018 or info@skyhorsepublishing.com.

Skyhorse® and Skyhorse Publishing® are registered trademarks of Skyhorse Publishing, Inc.®, a Delaware corporation.

www.skyhorsepublishing.com

10 9 8 7 6 5 4 3 2 1

Library of Congress Cataloging-in-Publication Data

Klinger, Ron.
 Bridge basics : a beginner's guide / by Ron Klinger. -- 6th ed.
    p. cm.
 ISBN 978-1-61608-233-8 (pbk. : alk. paper)
 1. Contract bridge. I. Title.
 GV1282.3.K6195 2011
 795.41'3--dc22
                                  2010039630

Printed in China

CONTENTS

Introduction for the Bridge Beginner

Bridge is fun to play, but the better you play the more fun it is. As you improve, you will be fascinated by how much there is to the game. Despite popular opinion to the contrary, bridge is not difficult to learn.

This book is the product of many classes given to beginners and improving players. It is intended for those who know nothing about bridge and also for those who already know how the game is played but wish to learn Standard American bidding or to improve their game. The book is set up to be used as a self-teacher or in conjunction with bridge classes.

If you are an absolute beginner, play through the games for beginners which are set out in Appendix 1, "From Whist to Bridge." After you have become familiar with the mechanics of the game, proceed to Chapter 1.

For the reader who can already play, do not try to memorize everything as you go, but do pay close attention to the examples, the exercises, the partnership bidding practice, and the play hands in each chapter. It is worth rereading the text every six months or so until you are confident you know all of the contents. It is beneficial to test yourself on the exercises as you go. These exercises simulate countless ordinary bidding situations, and by scoring well on the exercises you will build confidence and also score well at the table when everyday problems occur.

This book is not for the expert and will not make you an expert bridge player. It does not deal with expert bidding, expert play, or expert defense, but it does cover the ordinary, standard situations—*the basics* that make up over 95 percent of the game—where many players often go wrong. Follow the recommendations and you will eliminate fundamental flaws from your game and progress from a novice to a competent, confident bridge player.

To improve, you should try to play as often as possible, for the more you play, the speedier your improvement. It is all very well to take lessons and read books, but a lot of bridge competence is based on experience. The more often you encounter a basic situation, the more readily you will be able to deal with it in future.

Above all, remember that *bridge is a game to be enjoyed*. It can, and should, be a lot of fun and that is how you must approach it. I hope you derive as much enjoyment and satisfaction from it as I have.

Happy bridging.

Ron Klinger, 1972, 1991, 1993, 2000, 2011

Introduction for the Bridge Teacher

In conducting regular courses for bridge players, you will encounter two distinct groups in classes for beginners: those who have never played bridge (and may never have played cards), and those who have played before and might have learned the game socially, but who either know very little about bidding methods or have not played for quite some time and have forgotten most of what they have learned. It is quite a task to cater to both groups within one class. If you dwell at length on the basic concepts of a "trick," "trumps," "lead," and so on—needed for the absolute beginners—the more advanced players are wasting their time since they already know these fundamentals. On the other hand, if you cater to the advanced members of your class, you run a far greater risk of leaving the absolute beginners floundering, and they may lose interest and perhaps even give up.

Bridge Basics is suitable for classes for beginners' to improvers' standard. It is based on Standard American bidding and can be used for courses for absolute beginners. When dealing with absolute beginners, it is desirable to base the first class on "From Whist to Bridge" (Appendix 1) before starting on Chapter 1. This is like a "pre-bridge" course. It is even sensible to hold two such pre-bridge classes (for those who have never played) before commencing the course proper (when those who have played previously should join in).

Bridge Basics commences with the basics of all standard systems— the high card point count valuation and hand patterns. Chapter 2 covers the one-level suit opening bids. Page 28 is suitable if you are teaching 5-card majors. Use page 27 if you wish to teach 4-card suits.

Chapter 3 deals with the 1NT opening and the treatment of balanced hand patterns, but does not include the 2NT and 3NT openings or slam bidding. These appear later to reduce the content at the start of the course. It is important not to overwhelm your students with too much detail at the beginning.

The suit openings when holding a 5-card or longer suit are standard (open the longest suit, with 5-5 open the higher) regardless of which approach is adopted. Differences arise only for the 4-4-3-2, 4-3-3-3, and 4-4-4-1 patterns. Simply instruct your students to follow either page 27 or page 28. The answers to the exercises at the back of the book indicate when a difference arises because of the bidding system. However, the play hands have been constructed to tally with either method. Each teacher can thus cover the approach that is in local common usage.

Weak responding hands (under 10 points) are covered in Chapter 4 followed by strong responding hands (10 points or more) in Chapter 5. This division should simplify matters for both teacher and student. When we respond to a partner's opening, we think in terms of "weak hand" or "strong hand." This conceptual approach should be of considerable assistance to students. Bidding by a passed hand is covered in Chapter 6 and strong openings (2-openings plus 2NT and 3NT openings are discussed in Chapter 7). Slam bidding has a chapter of its own (Chapter 8), as do pre-emptive openings (Chapter 9). Each chapter has its own set of exercises, partnership bidding practices, and play hands.

The last three chapters deal with competitive bidding: overcalls, takeout doubles, and penalty doubles respectively. In the chapter on takeout doubles, the suit response at the cheapest level is 0-9 (counting distribution) and the jump-response is 10-12. The no-trump responses also conform to these ranges: the 1NT response to a double is 6-9 and the jump to 2NT is 10-12. The advantages of these ranges are that they coincide with the ranges for responding to an opening bid (0-5, 6-9, 10, or more) covered in the earlier chapters, and that the ranges for the no-trump responses dovetail with the ranges for a suit response. Both of these features mean that the ranges will strike students as familiar.

Students will not have to learn one set of ranges for suit bidding and a different one for no-trump responses.

The use of the 5-3-1 short suit count for suit responses to a takeout double has the effect of making the recommended ranges as accurate as necessary. The 3-2-1 short suit count is suggested as helpful in valuing a hand in order to make a takeout double, even if it is not used in determining when to open the bidding and when to pass.

The exercises, the partnership bidding, and the play hands provide more material than you can usually manage within a lesson. Choose the exercises you feel are most useful, but remember, the more student participation, the better. In particular, do not omit the four play hands. Students often find this to be the most valuable part of the class. Exercises that you have not been able to cover in class can be set as homework and corrected at the start of the next class.

Suggested Structure of Bridge Courses

Course content will vary according to the number of classes available and the standard of the players. The following are possible suggestions but, of course, you may construct your own curriculum.

Content of Bridge Courses (chapters in *Bridge Basics* in parentheses)

Absolute Beginners
12-week Course:
1. Whist to Bridge I (p. 119)
2. Whist to Bridge II (p. 123)
3. Basics & Suit Openings (1, 2)
4. 1NT Opening (3)
5. Weak Responding Hands (4)
6. Strong Responding Hands (5, 6)
7. Two-openings (7)
8. Slam Bidding (8)
9. Pre-empts (9)

10. Overcalls (10)
11. Doubles (11, 12)
12. Revision and Play Practice

10-week Course:
1. Whist to Bridge I (p. 119)
2. Whist to Bridge II (p. 123)
3. Basics & Suit Openings (1, 2)
4. 1NT Opening (3)
5. Weak Responding Hands (4)
6. Strong Responding Hands (5, 6)

7. Two-openings (7)
8. Slam Bidding (8)
9. Overcalls (10)
10. Doubles (11, 12)

8-week Course:
1. Whist to Bridge (p. 119)
2. Basics & Suit Openings (1, 2)
3. 1NT Openings (3)
4. Weak Responding Hands (4)
5. Strong Responding Hands (5, 6)
6. Two-openings (7)
7. Slam Bidding (8)
8. Overcalls, Doubles (10, 11)

Improvers
12-week Course:
1. Basics & Suit Openings (1, 2)
2. 1NT Opening (3)
3. Weak Responding Hands I (4)
4. Weak Responding Hands II (4)
5. Strong Responding Hands I (5)
6. Strong Responder II (5, 6)
7. Two-openings (7)
8. Slam Bidding (8)
9. Pre-empts (9)

10. Overcalls (10)
11. Doubles (11, 12)
12. Revision and Play Practice

10-week Course:
1. Basics & Suit Openings (1, 2)
2. 1NT Opening (3)
3. Weak Responding Hands (4)
4. Strong Responding Hands (5, 6)
5. Two-openings (7)
6. Slam Bidding (8)
7. Pre-empts (9)
8. Overcalls (10)
9. Doubles (11, 12)
10. Revision and Play Practice

8-week Course:
1. Basics & Opening Bids (1, 2, 3)
2. Weak Responding Hands (4)
3. Strong Responding Hands (5, 6)
4. Two-openings (7)
5. Slam Bidding (8)
6. Pre-empts (9)
7. Overcalls (10)
8. Doubles (11, 12)

Each of our classes lasts about two-and-one-half hours and the content of each class after the first follows this structure: correct homework, introduce new material, exercises, partnership bidding hands, coffee break, and play hands.

We do not spend much time on the homework, but it allows stragglers to come to class without missing any new material. Students bring their *Bridge Basics* to each class for partnership bidding and the play hands.

Make sure to include the four play hands in each class. They are at least as important as the main part of the lesson. Students learn much more quickly by playing than by listening and it is also more enjoyable. The hands are structured so that each player is declarer once. Except for the hands on defensive play (Chapter 10), each contract can be made and the idea is to give relatively new players confidence in their ability. After the cards have been sorted out, the students should be allowed to bid the hands themselves. After their bidding is finished, go over the bidding with the class and explain any traps or errors.

The final contract should be the one in the book, not some other contract the students might have reached. The opening lead is made and, if wrong, should be corrected together with an appropriate explanation. The students should be left to play the hands on their own, though some brief advice can be given (e.g., "You need to ruff a club in dummy."). Students should be encouraged to play the cards in duplicate fashion, so that the hand can be conveniently replayed, if necessary. After the hand, spend a little time explaining the main thrust of the hand, but remember that the students can go over the hands at home.

At the end of the course, encourage your students to play as often as possible. If you can arrange supervised practice sessions in conjunction with the course, so much the better. The aim of *Bridge Basics* is to make the game easy and fun for the students. If you can do the same, you will find that teaching bridge is a pleasant and rewarding pastime.

Ron Klinger, 1972, 1991, 1993, 2000

Changes in the 2011 sixth edition: The 1NT range is 15–17, the 2NT opening is 21–22, and 2♣: 2♦, 2NT caters for 23–24 balanced. The jump-raise of opener's suit is now a limit raise, 10–12 points. With more, the delayed game-raise is recommended.

Ron Klinger, 2011

Chapter 1
The Basics of All Standard Systems

THE HIGH CARD POINT COUNT

All standard systems start hand valuation by counting the high card content of the hand on this scale:

$$A = 4$$
$$K = 3$$
$$Q = 2$$
$$J = 1$$

These are known as High Card Points, or HCP. Other points may be added to the high card point total of the cards you hold, but all hand valuation starts with the 4-3-2-1 count. The first thing you will do after you have sorted your cards into suits is to count and total your high card points. Then you will move on to noting the shape of the hand and the number of cards in each suit.

HAND PATTERNS AND HAND SHAPES

Each bridge hand contains thirteen cards. The pattern of a hand describes the length of each suit in the hand starting with the longest suit, followed by the next longest and ending with the shortest. For example, to say that a hand is a 5-4-2-2 means that it contains a 5-card suit, a 4-card suit, plus two doubletons, while a 6-3-3-1 pattern means that the hand has a 6-card suit, two 3-card suits, and a singleton.

There are three hand shapes: balanced, semi-balanced, and unbalanced. A balanced hand has a 4-3-3-3, 4-4-3-2, or 5-3-3-2 pattern. It contains no void, no singleton, and at most one doubleton.

A semi-balanced hand has a 5-4-2-2, 6-3-2-2, or 7-2-2-2 pattern. It has no void, no singleton, but will have two or three doubletons (in contrast to the balanced shapes which contain either one doubleton or no doubleton).

Unbalanced hands consist of every other possible pattern, but they all have one common feature: they must contain a void or a singleton.

The hand shapes are summarized in the following table:

	HAND SHAPES	
BALANCED	**SEMI-BALANCED**	**UNBALANCED**
4-3-3-3	5-4-2-2	5-4-3-1
4-4-3-2	6-3-2-2	5-5-2-1
5-3-3-2	7-2-2-2	and all other shapes
No void, no singleton, at most one doubleton	No void, no singleton, two or three doubletons	which include a void or a singleton

Balanced hands are best for no-trump contracts. Since there is no very short suit, and at most one doubleton, there is little prospect for trumping and you are bound to follow suit almost throughout the hand. Therefore, a trump contract holds little attraction. Your approach would be to suggest no-trumps early in the bidding.

Unbalanced hands are best for trump contracts. As you hold either a void or a singleton, there is ample opportunity for trumping. Your best approach is to suggest one or more trump suits, reverting to no-trumps only as a last resort.

Semi-balanced hands are reasonable both for trump contracts and for no-trumps. There are two or three doubletons and that makes trumping attractive, while the absence of any singletons or voids makes no-trumps less risky.

1-SUITERS, 2-SUITERS, AND 3-SUITERS

Hands are also described according to how many suits are available for bidding. For a suit to be biddable, it requires at least four cards. When a hand contains only one suit with four or more cards, it is called a 1-suiter. When it contains two such suits, it is a 2-suiter and with three such suits, it is termed a 3-suiter. For example:

♠ 8 6 2	♠ A J 8 7 3	♠ A Q 7 6
♥ A 9 4	♥ K 4	♥ A K J 4
♦ A Q 9 8 3	♦ 8 2	♦ 9
♣ 5 4	♣ A Q J 9	♣ K Q J 9

This is a 10-point, balanced 1-suiter. Pattern: 5-3-3-2	15-point, semi-balanced 2-suiter. Pattern: 5-4-2-2	This is a 20-point, unbalanced 3-suiter. Pattern: 4-4-4-1

Exercise 1: Hand Shape

Hands can be balanced, semi-balanced, or unbalanced (see previous page). What is the shape of each of these hands?

1. ♠ x x x x	2. ♠ x x x x x	3. ♠ x x x x	4. ♠ x x
♥ x	♥ x	♥ x x	♥ x x x
♦ x x x x	♦ x x	♦ x x	♦ x x x
♣ x x x x	♣ x x x x x	♣ x x x x x	♣ x x x x x

5. ♠ x x x	6. ♠ x x x x	7. ♠ x x x	8. ♠ x x x x
♥ x x x x	♥ x x x x	♥ x	♥ x x x x
♦ x x x	♦ x x x	♦ x x x x	♦ x x x x
♣ x x x	♣ x x	♣ x x x x x	♣ x

Exercise 2: Points, Shape, and Hand Patterns

For each of the following hands, complete these details:

A. High Card Points   **B.** Shape   **C.** Pattern   **D.** 1-, 2-, or 3-suiter

1. ♠ A 4	2. ♠ A K 4 2	3. ♠ A 9 3	4. ♠ K J 8 7 6
♥ Q 8 6 3 2	♥ A 9 8 3	♥ Q 9 7 2	♥ A K J 6 3
♦ K Q J 9	♦ K 6	♦ A Q 4	♦ 6
♣ J 2	♣ 10 4 2	♣ Q 8 2	♣ J 8
A.	A.	A.	A. ....
B.	B.	B.	B. ....
C.	C.	C.	C. ....
D.	D.	D.	D. ....

5. ♠ K J	6. ♠ A K 9 4 2	7. ♠ A 10 9 6	8. ♠ 9 8 6 5 4 2
♥ 7 5 3	♥ - - -	♥ 5	♥ - - -
♦ A J 9 8 4 2	♦ 6 5	♦ K J 10 9	♦ A K 3
♣ Q 6	♣ A J 8 7 5 2	♣ A Q 10 5	♣ A Q 8 5
A.	A.	A.	A. ....
B.	B.	B.	B. ....
C.	C.	C.	C. ....
D.	D.	D.	D. ....

Points Needed for Games and Slams

IN ORDER TO MAKE		YOU + PARTNER NEED
3NT	9 tricks	26 points
4 Hearts or 4 Spades	10 tricks	26 points + 8 or more trumps
5 Clubs or 5 Diamonds	11 tricks	29 points + 8 or more trumps
6-in-a-suit	12 tricks	33 points + 8 or more trumps
7-in-a-suit	13 tricks	37 points + 8 or more trumps

To say that 26 points or more are required to make a game in 3NT or that 33 points are needed before you should try for a small slam does not automatically guarantee that you will succeed if you have that number of points. However, the point requirements do mean that with the indicated number of points, you are more likely to succeed than fail. Skill in declarer play may still be required, but even with skill you may fail if the cards lie badly for your side. Bridge is not a game of guarantees and certainties; it is a game in which one takes calculated risks. The point requirements reveal when the risks are worth taking—when the odds of obtaining a significant score are in your favor. Successful players are generally those who are prepared to "have a go" at game or slams.

If you and your partner have enough strength to make a game, but you fail to bid it, you have lost a valuable score. Similarly, if the partnership hands can produce a slam, but slam is not bid, again a valuable score is lost.

If the opposition bid and make a game, while you could have bid higher than their contract (even though you would have been defeated), you would have been better off to bid higher if the penalty for defeat would have been less than the value of their game. It is better to accept a small loss (a "sacrifice") than to let the opposition score a game or a slam.

You need not succeed in every game or every slam you bid. The rewards for games and slams are so great that failing now and again is no tragedy. A failure rate in games or slams of about 1 in 4 is normal and expected. Suppose that you bid to 3NT four times and fail on two occasions but succeed on two occasions. Your success rate is only 50 percent but you are some 700 points in front because of the bonus points for winning two games. The point to remember is that you need not be downhearted if you do not make every contract you bid.

TALKING BRIDGE

A little girl is watching her mother and three other ladies playing bridge. As the girl is taking a keen interest in the game, one of the ladies asks her, "And can you play bridge?" The girl replies, "No, but I can speak it."

Bridge players love to discuss bridge hands and there is an accepted method of description. To give a general account of the hand, state the number of high card points held and the hand pattern. For example:

♠ A J 8
♥ 7 3 2
♦ A K Q 9 5 3
♣ Q

A general description would be "A 16-point 6-3-3-1 hand." A more precise description details the pattern by suit lengths in the order of the suits: spades, hearts, diamonds, and clubs. Such a description of this hand would be "I held a 16-point, 3-3-6-1 . . ."

Most players, however, prefer to include the details of the actual high cards held. This is done by stating the honor cards in each suit followed by the total number of cards in that suit. Thus, A-9-6 is "ace to three," K-Q-5-2 is "king-queen to four," and A-K-J-8-4-2 is "ace-king-jack to six." Players in other parts of the world do use slightly different jargon, such as A-9-6 as "ace third," K-Q-5-2 as "king-queen fourth," and A-K-J-8-4-2 as "ace-king-jack sixth." Where the suit contains no honor cards, the number of cards in the suit is followed by the word "rags." Thus, 8-6-2 would be "three rags" and 9-7-4-3-2 is "five rags."

If a doubleton is held, use "doubleton" rather than "to two." Two specific cards (K-J) would be "king-jack doubleton," but where the suit has no honor, use "two rags," "rag doubleton," or "doubleton rag." Where a singleton is held, the terminology is the honor followed by singleton (such as "king singleton") or, with no honor, "singleton rag." It is also common to refer to a singleton honor as "bare" (such as "the bare king" or "king bare"). Slang for singleton is "stiff," so that king singleton becomes "stiff king" and a worthless singleton is simply "stiff."

The word "tight" is commonly used to mean "no more cards in the suit" so that king singleton is "king tight," K-Q doubleton is "king-queen tight," and so on. Specific cards followed by a worthless card are denoted by the word "another" to mean "and one worthless card." Thus, K-3 becomes "king-another," A-Q-J-4 is "ace-queen-jack-another," and so on.

The hand on page 22 could be described as "ace-jack to three, three rags, ace-king-queen sixth, and stiff queen."

BRIDGE NOTATION

When writing about bridge, it is conventional to write a bridge bid with the number first, denomination second, just as though it were spoken. Thus, 1NT stands for One No-Trump, 3♠ means Three Spades, 4♥ is a bid of Four Hearts, and so on. When writing about cards held or played, the suit symbol is written first followed by the card(s), so that ♠7 stands for the seven of spades, ♥K means the king of hearts, and so on.

When writing a bidding sequence, a colon (:) separates the bids. Bids by your side are written without parentheses and bids made by the opposing side are written inside parentheses; for example, 1♠ : (2♣) : Pass : (3♣) . . . When written bidding is in use, a diagonal stroke (/) indicates a pass, double is X, and redouble is XX.

STANDARD BIDDING SYSTEMS

A bidding system is like a language—it is a means of communicating with your partner. However, the language of bridge allows only fifteen legal words: one, two, three, four, five, six, seven, no-trumps, spades, hearts, diamonds, clubs, double, redouble, and pass ("no bid"). Without any opposition bidding, there are only thirty-five bids available between 1 Club and 7 No-Trumps. With this restricted language, you try to describe to your partner your thirteen cards, one of billions of possible hands.

Just as there are many languages, so there are many bidding systems. Just as some people are fluent in more than one language, so too are top players adept at more than one system. As some languages are easier to learn than others, so some bidding systems are more efficient than others.

A bidding system is not just one system. It consists of quite a number of subsystems, each dependent on which opening bid is chosen. The requirements to open the bidding, which opening bid is to be chosen, the requirements to respond, and what is meant by each possible response or rebid are stipulated by the system being learned. Just as words have different meanings in different languages, in different countries or in different ages, so bids frequently have different meanings in different systems.

Bridge Basics uses the world's most popular bidding system, Standard American. When you are just starting out at bridge, learn one basic system thoroughly and play it regularly for some two to three years. Only when you have become proficient in your system, and in general play, should you consider adopting some other system.

PART 1

STANDARD AMERICAN STYLE

5-CARD MAJORS, BETTER MINOR

or

MODERN STANDARD WITH 4-CARD SUITS

or

THE GOREN SYSTEM WITH 4-CARD SUITS

In this part you will learn:
- When to open the bidding and when to pass
- Which suit to start when you make a suit opening
- When to open with 1NT and when to prefer a suit opening
- When to start with a 1-opening and when to prefer a 2-opening
- How to respond to your partner's opening:
  - When to choose a suit response, when to prefer a no-trump response, and when to raise your partner's suit; when to respond at the cheapest level and when to make a jump-response; which suit to choose for your response when you have a choice of suits.
- How to choose your rebids as opener or responder
- How to judge when you should bid for game and when to stop low, when to try for slam and when to be satisfied with game.

Chapter 2
Opening with 1-in-a-suit

Turn to page 28 if you wish to learn 5-card Major openings.

(A) 4-card Suits—The Goren System
When valuing for a suit opening, count high card points and add:

Length Points
1 point for each 5-card suit, 2 points for a 6-card suit, and so on.

When Should You Open?
0–12 points: Do not open the bidding (but with 12 HCP you may open).
13–21 points: Open with 1-in-a-suit unless the hand fits a 1NT opening.
The one-opening should contain at least 10 high card points.
22 points or more: Choose a 2-opening (see Chapter 7).

Which Suit Should You Open?
(1) Open your longest suit. Bid a 6-card minor ahead of a 5-card major.
(2) With two 5-card suits or two 6-card suits, open the higher-ranking.
(3) With two or three 4-card suits, open the 4-card suit below your
shortage. Locate your shortest suit (singleton or doubleton) and go
down in rank and bid the first 4-card suit below your shortest suit.
Longest first; 5-5 / 6-6: higher first; 4-carders: below-the-shortage.

Biddable Suits and the Convenient Club
Any 5-card or longer suit may be opened. Any 4-card minor
may be opened. To open a 4-card major, the suit should contain at

least 4 points. If not, you are permitted to open 1♣ with a 3-card club suit.

(B) 4-CARD SUITS—MODERN STANDARD

This is exactly the same as above except when it comes to (3), opening with no 5-card or longer suit:

(3) With two or three 4-card suits, open the cheapest 4-card suit. This is bidding your suits "up-the-line." Five-card suits are bid "down-the-line" (higher suit first) and 4-card suits are bid "up-the-line" (cheapest first).

Longest first; 5-5 or 6-6: higher first; 4-carders: up-the-line.

The same rules apply when you are responder with a choice of suits.

Biddable Suits

Any 4-card suit may be opened. Any 5-card suit may be bid twice.

(C) 5-CARD MAJORS, BETTER MINOR

This is the most popular modern style.

When valuing for a suit opening, count high card points and add:

LENGTH POINTS

1 point for each 5-card suit, 2 points for a 6-card suit, and so on.

When Should You Open?

0–11 points: Do not open with a one-bid. With a long, strong suit, your hand may be worth a pre-emptive opening of 3, 4, or 5 (see Chapter 9).

12 HCP: Open the bidding unless your hand pattern is 4-3-3-3.

12 total points but only 11 HCP or less (or 12 HCP with a 4-3-3-3 pattern): Do not open with a one-bid.

13–21 points: Open with one-in-a-suit unless your hand fits a 1NT opening. The one-opening should contain at least 10 high card points.

22 points or more: Choose a two-opening (see Chapter 7).

Which Suit Should You Open?

(1) Open the longest suit. Bid a 6-card minor ahead of a 5-card major.

(2) With two 5-card suits or two 6-card suits, open the higher-ranking.

(3) With no 5-card suit, open the longer minor.

- Do not open 1♠ or 1♥ in first or second seat unless you have at least five cards in that suit.
- With 4-4 in the minors, open 1♦ (which will almost always be a 4-card suit and so you can raise diamonds with 4-card support).
- With 3-3 in the minors, open 1♣.
- There is no minimum suit quality for an opening bid. The opening bid chosen depends solely on the length of the suits.

EXAMPLES

1.	2.	3.	4.
♠ A J 9 4 2	♠ A J 8	♠ K J 9 6	♠ J 8 4 3
♥ A	♥ K Q 9 6	♥ 7	♥ A Q 6
♦ Q J 7 4 3 2	♦ K 8 4 3	♦ Q 8 4 3	♦ A J 7
♣ 5	♣ J 8	♣ A K 9 8	♣ Q 5 2
Open 1♦.	Open 1♦.	Open 1♦.	Open 1♣.
Longest first.	Longer minor.	4-4 minors.	3-3 minors.

There is very little difference playing 5-card majors or 4-card suits. The differences arise when opening the bidding with no 5-card suit and the support needed to raise your partner (3+ cards = support for a 5-card suit and 4+ cards = support for a 4-card suit). The rest is the same.

EXERCISE ON OPENING THE BIDDING

You are the dealer, neither side is vulnerable. What action do you take?
Answers are supplied for 5-card Majors and for 4-card Suits systems.

1.	♠ A Q 7 ♥ K Q 8 6 ♦ 3 ♣ J 8 7 4 2	2.	♠ A Q 7 ♥ K Q 8 6 2 ♦ 3 ♣ J 8 7 4	3.	♠ A 8 7 ♥ K Q 8 6 2 ♦ 3 ♣ J 8 7 4	4.	♠ A 8 7 ♥ K Q 8 6 2 ♦ 3 ♣ A K Q 4
5.	♠ A K 7 6 3 ♥ A 3 ♦ 6 ♣ K Q 9 5 2	6.	♠ Q 9 8 6 2 ♥ A K J 7 3 ♦ J 5 ♣ 6	7.	♠ K Q J ♥ A 8 6 4 3 ♦ K Q 7 4 2 ♣ - - -	8.	♠ 8 ♥ A J 9 7 2 ♦ A Q J 8 4 3 ♣ 6
9.	♠ A J 9 ♥ K Q 7 ♦ J 8 4 3 ♣ J 7 2	10.	♠ A Q 9 ♥ K Q 7 ♦ J 8 4 3 ♣ J 7 2	11.	♠ A K 9 ♥ K J 7 ♦ A 4 3 ♣ K J 6 2	12.	♠ A Q 7 2 ♥ A 9 8 ♦ K 7 2 ♣ 9 8 4
13.	♠ A Q 7 4 ♥ J 8 7 ♦ 6 2 ♣ K Q 9 3	14.	♠ A K 8 ♥ Q 9 6 2 ♦ A 4 ♣ 6 4 3 2	15.	♠ 6 2 ♥ A J 8 ♦ K 9 7 2 ♣ A J 5 4	16.	♠ A K J 9 ♥ A Q 3 ♦ A 9 6 2 ♣ Q 8
17.	♠ A Q 7 2 ♥ K Q 9 3 ♦ Q 7 6 2 ♣ 4	18.	♠ A J 8 3 ♥ Q 7 4 2 ♦ 9 ♣ A Q J 2	19.	♠ A K 3 2 ♥ 7 ♦ A Q 4 3 ♣ A J 6 5	20.	♠ 9 ♥ A 8 7 6 ♦ K 9 4 3 ♣ A Q 7 2
21.	♠ K 9 7 6 2 ♥ A Q 3 ♦ Q 7 ♣ 8 6 5	22.	♠ A Q 9 7 6 2 ♥ K Q 3 ♦ 7 6 3 ♣ 4	23.	♠ A J 8 7 4 ♥ 4 ♦ A Q 9 6 5 ♣ 7 2	24.	♠ 8 7 ♥ A J 8 ♦ 6 4 2 ♣ A K 6 4 3
25.	♠ K J 9 4 ♥ A Q 8 5 ♦ Q 7 4 ♣ J 8	26.	♠ K J 9 4 ♥ A Q 8 5 ♦ Q 7 ♣ J 8 6	27.	♠ K J 9 ♥ 7 2 ♦ Q 8 4 3 ♣ A K 9 8	28.	♠ K J 9 ♥ 8 7 6 2 ♦ Q 8 3 ♣ A K 9

Play Hands on Opening with 1-in-a-suit

Hand 1: High-Cards-from-Shortage, Low-from-Length

Dealer North: Nil vulnerable

NORTH
♠ A Q J 7
♥ 9 4 3
♦ Q 7 5
♣ 6 4 2

WEST
♠ 6 5
♥ K Q J 10 8 2
♦ A 8
♣ J 8 5

EAST
♠ 10 9 4 3 2
♥ 5
♦ J 10 9 6
♣ K Q 10

SOUTH
♠ K 8
♥ A 7 6
♦ K 4 3 2
♣ A 9 7 3

WEST	NORTH	EAST	SOUTH
	Pass	Pass	1♦
1♥	1♠	Pass	1NT
Pass	Pass	Pass	

Lead: ♥ K. Top of sequence.

Correct play: After taking the ♥A, play the ♠K (high-from-shortage) followed by a spade to dummy and cash the other spade winners. Then lead a diamond to your king to set up a diamond trick. 7 tricks.

Wrong play: (1) Playing a low spade rather than the king first. (2) Cashing the ♣A before setting up a diamond trick. This would allow the defense to defeat the contract with hearts and clubs and the ♦A.

Hand 2: Overcalling—The High-Card-from-Shortage Principle

Dealer East: N-S vulnerable

NORTH
♠ Q 10 9 2
♥ 3 2
♦ J 6
♣ 9 8 7 5 4

WEST
♠ 8 7 6
♥ K 6
♦ 9 4 3
♣ A K Q J 2

EAST
♠ A J 3
♥ Q 5 4
♦ A K 5 2
♣ 10 6 3

SOUTH
♠ K 5 4
♥ A J 10 9 8 7
♦ Q 10 8 7
♣ - - -

WEST	NORTH	EAST	SOUTH
		1♦	1♥
2♣	Pass	2NT	Pass
3NT	Pass	Pass	Pass

Lead: ♥ J. With an interior sequence (starting in the middle of a suit), lead top of the cards that are in sequence.

Correct play: Win the first heart and start on the clubs, playing the 10 from hand and the 2 from dummy (high-from-shortage). Cash the clubs, the ace of spades and A-K of diamonds.

Wrong play: Failing to win with the 10 of clubs on the first or second round of clubs. This restricts you to just four club tricks because of the 5-0 split and you could go off.

Hand 3: Overtaking a Winner in Order to Reach Dummy

Dealer East: E-W vulnerable

WEST	NORTH	EAST	SOUTH
			Pass
1♦	Pass	1♠	Pass
1NT	Pass	2NT	Pass
3NT	Pass	Pass	Pass

NORTH
♠ 7 5 4 3
♥ Q J 10 9
♦ K Q 10
♣ 10 6

WEST
♠ Q J
♥ 6 3 2
♦ J 8 5 2
♣ A K Q J

EAST
♠ A K 10 2
♥ A 4
♦ 6 4 3
♣ 8 5 3 2

SOUTH
♠ 9 8 6
♥ K 8 7 5
♦ A 9 7
♣ 9 7 4

Lead: ♥Q. Top of sequence. With equal length, lead the stronger suit.

Correct play: Take the ♥A at once and lead a low spade to the queen (high-from-shortage), then ♠J, overtaking with dummy's king or ace. Cash the spade and club winners.

Wrong play: (1) Playing ♠A or ♠K on the first round of spades. (2) Failing to overtake the second round of spades with dummy's ace or king. This would leave two spade winners stranded in dummy.

Hand 4: Overtaking a Winner to Gain Access to Dummy

Dealer West: Both vulnerable

WEST	NORTH	EAST	SOUTH
Pass	1♣	Pass	1♦
Pass	1NT	Pass	3NT
Pass	Pass	Pass	

NORTH
♠ J 9 2
♥ A K 2
♦ K Q J
♣ 8 6 3 2

WEST
♠ A 6 4
♥ 10 9 8 5
♦ 8 4
♣ A 10 7 5

EAST
♠ 10 8 7 5 3
♥ Q 7 6
♦ 9 7 2
♣ K 9

SOUTH
♠ K Q
♥ J 4 3
♦ A 10 6 5 3
♣ Q J 4

Lead: ♠5, fourth-highest.

Correct play: West should win ♠A and return a spade. Lead a diamond to the king, cash the ♦Q and then play the ♦J, overtaking with dummy's ace. Cash the diamonds, the hearts and the jack of spades. 9 tricks.

Wrong play: (1) Failing to overtake the third round of diamonds. This allows the defense to defeat 3NT.
(2) Playing the ♦A on the first or second round of diamonds. This will "block" the diamonds and thus leave two diamond winners stranded in dummy.

Chapter 3

The 1NT Opening

The 1NT opening shows 15–17 points and balanced shape.

Most hands in the 13–21 zone start with a suit opening, but if your hand fits 1NT, prefer that opening to any other.

How to Handle Balanced Hands (4-4-3-2 / 5-3-3-2 / 4-3-3-3)

0–11 points: Pass

12 HCP: Open if 4-4-3-2 or 5-3-3-2. Pass in 1st or 2nd seat if 4-3-3-3.

13–14 points: Open with 1-in-a-suit (see Chapter 2).

15–17 points: Open 1NT with any balanced hand, that is, any 4-3-3-3, 4-4-3-2, or 5-3-3-2 pattern.

18–21 points: Open with 1-in-a-suit (see Chapter 2) except for:

21–22 balanced: Open 2NT. Others with 22+ points: See Chapter 7.

Winning Strategy:

When holding 26 points or more between you and your partner, the partnership should bid a game.

Therefore, do not pass in the bidding until some game is reached if the partnership *could* have 26 points or more.

With 26 points together, game is a good chance.

With 25 points together, game is a reasonable chance.

With 24 points or less, game prospects are poor.

RESPONDING TO 1NT WITH A BALANCED HAND

0–7 points	PASS	Game prospects poor
8–9 points	2NT	Game prospects possible
10–14 points	3NT	Good chances for game
15 points or more	See Chapter 8	Slam is possible
Unbalanced hands	See Chapters 4 & 5	

After 1NT: 2NT, opener should pass with 15 points (minimum) and continue to 3NT with 16–17 points (maximum). After 1NT: 3NT, opener must pass. After a 1NT, 2NT, or 3NT opening, responder makes the decision how high to bid. Responder knows the combined strength; opener does not.

EXERCISES

A. What is your opening bid on these hands?

1.	2.	3.	4.
♠ A Q 6	♠ A Q 6	♠ A Q 6 4 3	♠ K J 6
♥ K Q 8	♥ K Q	♥ K Q	♥ A Q 9
♦ 7 6 5	♦ 7 6 5	♦ 7 6 5	♦ A 10 6 3
♣ A J 9 4	♣ A J 9 4 2	♣ A J 9	♣ K Q 8

B. Your partner opens 1NT. What is your response?

1.	2.	3.	4.
♠ A 9 8	♠ K 7 6	♠ K 7 6	♠ A K
♥ K J 7	♥ 4 3	♥ J 3	♥ 7 6 4
♦ Q 9 8 4	♦ K 9 8 2	♦ K Q 8 2	♦ Q 9 8
♣ 7 6 2	♣ 7 6 4 3	♣ 7 6 4 3	♣ K J 7 6 2

PARTNERSHIP BIDDING PRACTICE

West is the dealer on each hand. How should the bidding go?

	WEST		EAST		WEST		EAST
1.	♠ A J 7 2	1.	♠ K Q 9	5.	♠ 6 2	5.	♠ A Q 7
	♥ 7 6 4 3		♥ A 8		♥ Q 10 6		♥ K J 8 2
	♦ 7 5		♦ A K 8 4		♦ K Q J 4		♦ A 7 6
	♣ 8 7 2		♣ J 9 4 3		♣ 8 7 4 3		♣ K 9 5
2.	♠ K Q 8 6	2.	♠ A 3 2	6.	♠ A 3 2	6.	♠ Q 6 4
	♥ 9 4		♥ 10 8 6		♥ A 10 9 2		♥ 8 3
	♦ A Q J		♦ 9 6 3 2		♦ K Q 7 2		♦ J 10 5
	♣ K 7 6 2		♣ A 10 5		♣ K J		♣ Q 8 6 4 3
3.	♠ A J 4	3.	♠ K Q 6 3 2	7.	♠ A 3 2	7.	♠ Q J 6 5
	♥ 9 5 3		♥ A K		♥ 9 8 7		♥ A 6 2
	♦ J 10 6		♦ 8 7 4		♦ A Q 4		♦ 8 3 2
	♣ A 9 7 6		♣ K 8 2		♣ A K 6 5		♣ 9 4 3
4.	♠ A J 9 2	4.	♠ K Q 7	8.	♠ A 10 8	8.	♠ K 7 5
	♥ K Q J		♥ 8 4 2		♥ 9 2		♥ A 6 5 4
	♦ K 9 2		♦ A 6 5 3		♦ A 10 8 6 4		♦ K Q 9 3
	♣ Q 8 4		♣ 7 5 3		♣ Q 8 7		♣ A 5

PLAY HANDS FOR THE ONE NO-TRUMP OPENING
Hand 5: High-Cards-from-Shortage, Low-from-Length
Dealer North: Nil vulnerable

WEST	NORTH	EAST	SOUTH
	Pass	Pass	1NT
Pass	Pass	Pass	

NORTH
- ♠ A Q 5 3
- ♥ 8 6 3
- ♦ 7 4 2
- ♣ 10 8 5

WEST
- ♠ 7 6
- ♥ J 10 9
- ♦ 10 6 3
- ♣ A Q 9 7 4

EAST
- ♠ 10 9 8 2
- ♥ Q 5 4
- ♦ K Q J 9
- ♣ K 2

SOUTH
- ♠ K J 4
- ♥ A K 7 2
- ♦ A 8 5
- ♣ J 6 3

Lead: ♣7. Against no-trumps, lead your long suit. Choose the fourth-highest when no sequence of three or more cards is held.

Play: East plays the ♣K (third-hand-high), winning the trick, and returns a club. Return your partner's lead unless you have a very good alternative. The defenders win the first five tricks; South discarding red suit losers from both hands. Do not discard a spade. South wins the ♥J switch at trick 6 and cashes four spades, playing the king first, then the jack, then low to dummy.

Hand 6: The High-Card-from-Shortage Principle
Dealer North: Nil vulnerable

WEST	NORTH	EAST	SOUTH
		1NT	Pass
3NT	Pass	Pass	Pass

NORTH
- ♠ K 10 9 7 4
- ♥ 10
- ♦ 10 5 2
- ♣ 10 8 4 3

WEST
- ♠ Q J 2
- ♥ 8 6 5
- ♦ 7 6 4
- ♣ A K J 6

EAST
- ♠ 8 5 3
- ♥ A 4 3 2
- ♦ A K Q J
- ♣ Q 5

SOUTH
- ♠ A 6
- ♥ K Q J 9 7
- ♦ 9 8 3
- ♣ 9 7 2

Lead: ♥K. Top of the sequence.

Correct play: Win the ♥A, play the queen of clubs (high-from-shortage first), then the other clubs and the four diamonds. 3NT made.

Wrong play: (1) Playing the 5 of clubs to dummy's ace and next cashing the ♣K costs you the queen of clubs and you will fail by one trick. (2) Playing the ♣5 to a winner in dummy and the ♣6 to your queen leaves two club winners in dummy and no quick entry to reach them.

Hand 7: Overtaking a Winner in Order to Reach Dummy

Dealer South: E-W vulnerable

WEST	NORTH	EAST	SOUTH
			Pass
Pass	1NT	Pass	2NT
Pass	3NT	All pass	

NORTH
♠ Q 9 8
♥ 7 6 5 4
♦ A Q
♣ A K Q 6

WEST
♠ A 10 5 2
♥ 10 3 2
♦ 9 6 3
♣ 9 7 5

EAST
♠ K J 3
♥ K Q J 9
♦ 8 7 5 2
♣ J 10

SOUTH
♠ 7 6 4
♥ A 8
♦ K J 10 4
♣ 8 4 3 2

Lead: ♥ K. With equally long suits, lead the stronger. Top from sequence.

Correct play: After winning the ♥ A, lead a low diamond to the *ace* (high-from-shortage, low-from-length) and play ♦ Q, overtaking with dummy's king. Cash the diamond winners, followed by the clubs. 9 tricks.

Wrong play: (1) Winning the first round of diamonds with the queen. This "blocks" the diamonds. (2) Winning the first round of diamonds with the ace, but failing to overtake the ♦ Q with dummy's king.

Hand 8: Overtaking a Winner to Gain Access to Dummy

Dealer West: Both vulnerable

WEST	NORTH	EAST	SOUTH
1NT	Pass	Pass	Pass

NORTH
♠ 8 7 4
♥ Q 9 6
♦ Q 8
♣ K J 9 4 2

WEST
♠ A K J
♥ A 7 3
♦ A 5 4 2
♣ 10 8 7

EAST
♠ Q 10 3 2
♥ 8 5 4
♦ 9 6 3
♣ A 6 5

SOUTH
♠ 9 6 5
♥ K J 10 2
♦ K J 10 7
♣ Q 3

Lead: ♣ 4, fourth-highest.

Correct play: If a low card is played from dummy, South plays the ♣ Q (third-hand-high) and returns a club. After winning the ♣ A, declarer should play a spade to the ace (high-from-shortage), cash the ♠ K (high-from-shortage), and lead the ♠ J, overtaking with dummy's queen to cash the ♠ 10 next. Making 7 tricks.

Wrong play: (1) Playing the ♠ J on the first or second round of spades, thus "blocking" the spade suit. (2) Failing to overtake the ♠ J with dummy's queen on the third round of spades. The ♠ Q is now stranded.

Chapter 4
Responding with Weak Hands

RESPONDING TO AN OPENING OF 1♣, 1♦, 1♥, OR 1♠

- **0–5 points:** Pass
- **6–9 points:** Bid only at the 1-level *or* raise opener's suit to the 2-level.

An average hand contains 10 high card points. Hands below 10 points are considered weak, but game is still possible if your partner has a very strong hand. *Therefore, always respond to a suit opening bid with 6 points or more, but normally pass with a hand in the 0–5 point range.*

If responding with a weak hand, keep the bidding at a low level initially, since your partner may have only a minimum opening of 12–13 points. Then the partnership will have only about 20 points, perhaps a little more. With the strength evenly divided between the two sides, it will be tough to make more than 7 or 8 tricks. Consequently, you may raise opener's suit to the 2-level with a weak hand, but otherwise remain at the 1-level.

Do not bid a new suit at the 2-level with 6–9 points, only with 10 high card points or better, or with 11 or more points, including length points.

YOUR CHOICE OF RESPONSE:
RAISE OPENER *OR* NEW SUIT *OR* 1NT

Raise opener to the 2-level: 6–9 points + support for opener's suit.

A decent trump holding for your partnership is 8 trumps or more. With fewer than 8 trumps, the opponents will have almost as many, or more, than you, making your task to win very difficult. To ensure the partnership has at least 8 trumps, you should have three trumps (or more) to support a 5-card suit (an opening bid of 1 ♥ or 1 ♠ if playing 5-card majors), four trumps (or more) to support a 4-card suit, and five trumps (or more) to support a 1 ♣ opening if that suit that might be just a 3-carder.

Without support for your partner, count high card points and length points.

With support for your partner, ignore length points and count high card points plus Ruffing Points: 5 for a void, 3 for a singleton, 1 for each doubleton.

With 10 HCP and a 4-3-3-3 pattern with support for opener, a raise to the 2-level is acceptable. With less than 10 HCP but a total of 10 points after adding distribution, a raise to the 2-level is also acceptable.

Bid Your Own Suit (but only at the 1-level): 6 points or more.

The suit you bid must contain at least four cards, but it need not have any high cards in the suit itself. In other words, any 4-card suit is biddable for responder. A significant difference between bidding your own suit at the 1-level and raising opener to the 2-level or responding 1NT is this: While the raise is 6-9 and the 1NT response is 6-9, the new suit response is 6 points *or more*. In other words, a new suit at the 1-level might be based on a strong hand, which you will reveal later in the bidding, but it need not have more than the minimum of 6 points. Because the raise to the 2-level is limited (6-9) and the 1NT response is limited (6-9), opener may pass these responses, but because a new suit response has a very wide range (6 points or more), opener is obliged to rebid after a new suit response.

Where you have a choice of suits as responder, the order of preference is:

(1) Bid your longest suit first.

(2) With two 5-card suits or two 6-card suits, bid the higher-ranking.

(3) With two or three 4-card suits, bid the cheapest suit first.

"Cheapest" means the first available bid over your partner's bid, not necessarily the lowest-ranking suit. If your partner opened 1♥ and you have 4 spades and 4 clubs, 1♠ is a cheaper bid than 2♣. Likewise, if your partner opened 1♦ and you hold 4 spades and 4 hearts, the cheaper suit is hearts and your response should be 1♥. This method of bidding your cheapest 4-card suit is called bidding your suits "up-the-line." Note that the up-the-line rule applies only to 4-card suits, *not to 5-card suits.*

This order of preference in bidding suits is subject to the priority that *you should not bid a new suit at the 2-level unless you have at least 10 high card points (or 11 or more points including length points).*

Consequently, when you have only 6-9 points, you may occasionally be forced into bidding a suit which is not your normal first preference. Suppose your partner has opened 1♦ and you have 6 points with 4 spades and 5 clubs. You should respond 1♠. Your hand is not strong enough for 2♣.

Respond 1NT: 6–9 points, no support for opener, no suit that you can bid at the 1-level, *any shape.* If unable to raise opener and unable to bid a suit at the 1-level, respond 1NT as your last resort. Because of the importance of the rule requiring 10+ points for a new suit at the 2-level, *the 1NT response need not be balanced.* With 10 HCP and a 4-3-3-3 pattern, prefer a 1NT response to a 2-level change of suit.

RESOLVING A CHOICE OF RESPONSES

What happens when your hand fits two or more responses? Perhaps you are able to support your partner but you also have a suit of your own? Perhaps you could raise opener, bid your own suit, or respond 1NT? The way to solve such conflicts will depend on whether your partner has opened with a major suit or with a minor suit. If you have only 6–9 points, this is the order of priorities when responding:

If your partner opened with a major suit:
(1) Raise opener's major.
(2) Bid 1♠ over 1♥ if unable to support hearts.
(3) Respond 1NT.

If your partner opened with a minor suit:
(1) Change suit at the 1-level. Prefer a major to raising a minor.
(2) Raise opener's minor. It is better to raise opener's minor than to show the other minor.
(3) Respond 1NT.

These priorities apply when responding with a weak hand. There may be different priorities when responding with a strong hand.

When changing suit in response to an opening bid of 1♣ or 1♦, follow the normal rules when you have a choice of suits: longest suit first; the higher suit with two 5-card suits or two 6-card suits; bid up-the-line with 4-card suits.

EXERCISE

What is your response on these hands if your partner opened:

(a) 1 Club?   (b) 1 Diamond?   (c) 1 Heart?   (d) 1 Spade?

1.	♠ J 4 3 2 ♥ 8 6 ♦ A J 7 4 3 ♣ 9 5	2.	♠ K J 8 3 ♥ Q 5 4 2 ♦ 7 6 ♣ 8 7 3	3.	♠ Q J 6 5 2 ♥ K 3 ♦ 8 7 3 ♣ 9 4 2	4.	♠ 9 8 4 2 ♥ 7 4 ♦ A 8 5 ♣ A 8 3 2
5.	♠ A Q 8 3 ♥ 8 7 6 2 ♦ 7 5 ♣ 4 3 2	6.	♠ K 9 7 4 3 ♥ 6 ♦ A 7 6 5 4 2 ♣ 4	7.	♠ 4 3 ♥ A J 7 6 ♦ 6 2 ♣ Q J 7 5 4	8.	♠ 4 3 ♥ Q 9 7 5 4 ♦ 9 8 6 4 ♣ 3 2

EXERCISES ON RESPONDING WITH A WEAK HAND

A. Your partner opens 1♣, next player passes. What is your response?

1.	♠ K J 8 ♥ A 7 6 ♦ 9 6 4 ♣ 8 7 3 2	2.	♠ K J 8 ♥ A 7 6 ♦ 9 6 4 3 ♣ 8 7 3	3.	♠ K J 8 ♥ A 7 6 4 ♦ 9 6 4 ♣ 8 7 3	4.	♠ K J 8 2 ♥ A 7 6 ♦ 9 6 4 ♣ 8 7 3
5.	♠ A 7 4 2 ♥ 7 6 ♦ K 8 6 4 ♣ 9 4 3	6.	♠ A 7 4 2 ♥ K 8 6 4 ♦ 7 6 ♣ 9 4 3	7.	♠ A 7 4 2 ♥ 7 6 ♦ 9 4 3 ♣ K 8 6 4	8.	♠ 7 6 ♥ K 8 6 4 ♦ A 7 4 2 ♣ 9 4 3
9.	♠ A 8 6 3 2 ♥ Q J 7 6 5 ♦ 9 ♣ 7 2	10.	♠ A 8 6 3 2 ♥ 9 ♦ 7 2 ♣ Q J 7 6 5	11.	♠ K J 7 5 ♥ J 8 4 3 ♦ Q 9 8 3 ♣ 2	12.	♠ K J 7 5 ♥ J 8 4 3 ♦ 2 ♣ Q 9 8 3
13.	♠ A J 7 2 ♥ 7 6 ♦ 5 4 ♣ Q 9 8 6 3	14.	♠ 7 6 ♥ 5 4 ♦ A J 7 2 ♣ Q 9 8 6 3	15.	♠ Q 6 ♥ 5 4 2 ♦ A J 7 ♣ 9 8 6 3 2	16.	♠ Q J 7 2 ♥ 6 ♦ A 9 7 6 4 3 ♣ 5 2

B. Your partner opens 1♥, next player passes. What is your response?

1. ♠ K 7 6 4
   ♥ 8
   ♦ Q 9 7 2
   ♣ Q 8 4 3

2. ♠ 8 7 5 3
   ♥ 9 2
   ♦ J 8 4 3
   ♣ A K 2

3. ♠ K 7 4
   ♥ 8 6
   ♦ A J 7 4
   ♣ 9 5 3 2

4. ♠ Q J 9 4
   ♥ 8
   ♦ A J 8 6 3
   ♣ 7 6 2

5. ♠ A 7
   ♥ J 7 6 3
   ♦ 9 8 7 4
   ♣ 4 3 2

6. ♠ A J 7 2
   ♥ Q 9 8 3
   ♦ 7 6 4
   ♣ 4 2

7. ♠ A J 7 3 2
   ♥ Q 8 7 5
   ♦ 7 5
   ♣ 4 2

8. ♠ Q J 9
   ♥ 6
   ♦ Q 9 7 4
   ♣ K 7 5 3 2

9. ♠ 9 4 3 2
   ♥ 8
   ♦ A K J 3
   ♣ 9 5 3 2

10. ♠ 8 3
    ♥ 6 2
    ♦ K 8 4 3 2
    ♣ Q J 6 4

11. ♠ J 2
    ♥ 8 6
    ♦ A J 8 6 4 3
    ♣ Q 9 5

12. ♠ 7
    ♥ K 9 8 2
    ♦ 7 5 4 3
    ♣ J 8 5 2

Shut-out Jump-raises

The jump-raises to game in the major suits (1♥: 4♥ and 1♠: 4♠) are used on weakish responding hands. They show about 6-9 high card points (could even be less), excellent trump support (more than the minimum needed for a raise), and unbalanced shape (must have a singleton or a void). The message is: "I have excellent support, but am weak in high cards." They are called "shut-out" because their function is to shut the next player out of the bidding. At the same time they serve as a warning to your partner not to expect too much in high cards if your partner has notions about a slam. They are also known as "weak freaks" or "gambling raises," but with the excellent support and unbalanced shape, it is not much of a gamble.

Shut-out raises in minor suits are also available (1♣: 4♣ *or* 1♣: 5♣ *or* 1♦: 4♦ *or* 1♦: 5♦), but these are very rare since they bypass a potential 3NT contract. When used, however, they do show the same sort of hand as the shut-out raise in the major suits, namely, weak in high cards (often 6-9 high card points, but they can be much weaker), 5-card or longer trump support, and an unbalanced hand (it has to contain a void or a singleton).

Responding to an Opening Bid of 1NT

Responding to 1NT with a balanced hand was covered in Chapter 3. Responding to 1NT with a weak, unbalanced hand is different to responding to a suit opening, because the 1NT opening is closely defined, a balanced 15-17, while the suit opening has a wide range, 12–21 points with balanced, semi-balanced, or unbalanced shape. You would pass a suit opening with 0–5 points, but you are allowed, even encouraged, to respond to 1NT with a hopelessly weak hand, provided that you have a long suit:

1NT: 2-in-a-suit = 0–7 points and a 5-card or longer suit. Opener should pass this 2-level response, but with 17 points and 4-card support, opener is permitted to raise responder's suit to the 3-level.

1NT: 2♣ is commonly used as the Stayman Convention which you should certainly adopt after playing for some time (see page 127).

With 8 points or more, responder has a chance for game opposite 1NT and therefore must not make a weak suit response at the 2-level. 2NT is used as a response with exactly 8–9 points (see Chapter 3) and the Stayman Convention (see page 127) can also be used when exploring for game in a major suit with 8 points or more. Other strong responses to 1NT are covered in Chapter 5.

OPENER'S REBIDS AFTER A WEAK RESPONSE

Opener's hand is generally divided into three ranges:

12–15 points:	Minimum opening
16–18 points:	Strong opening
19 points up:	Maximum opening

Strategy: If the partnership may hold 26 points, keep on bidding since game is feasible. If the combined total is 25 points at least and there might be more, bid for a game. If the combined total is 25 points at most and there might be less, do not bid for a game. With 26 points together, game is a good bet; with 25 points together, game is a reasonable bet, and with 24 points or less together, game is a poor bet. This bidding strategy is revealed in the approach taken by opener after a weak response from partner.

Opener's Action after a Raise to the 2-level (e.g., 1♥: 2♥, ... ?)

Count HCP Plus 5-3-1 Shortages (void 5, singleton 3, doubleton 1).

12–15 points	**Pass.** Responder has 6-9, so no 26 points together.
16–18 points	**Bid again.** Raise a major to the 3-level; if your suit is a minor, raise to the 3-level or try 2NT.
19 points up	**Bid game.** If your suit is a major, raise to the 4-level; if it is a minor, consider 3NT if your hand is balanced or semi-balanced.

After a 1NT Response (e.g., 1♦ : 1NT, . . . ?)

(a) If satisfied with no-trumps:

12–15 points	**Pass.** Responder has 6-9, so no 26 points together.
16–18 points	**2NT.** Opener figures to be semi-balanced.
19 points up	**3NT.** The partnership has 25 points at worst.

(b) If not happy with no-trumps:

12–15 points	Bid a new suit lower than your first bid suit *or* repeat your first suit with extra length in the suit.
16–18 points	Bid any new suit *or* with no second suit, jump to three in the first suit with six or more cards in it.
19 points up	Jump to the 3-level in a new suit (jump-shift) *or* jump to game in your suit.

♠ A 9 8 4 3 ♥ A 9 7 ♦ K Q ♣ J 3 2	You opened 1♠. Your rebid after 2♠ or 1NT? Over 2♠ you should pass—the partnership does not have 26 points. Pass also over 1NT. With a 5-3-3-2, the shape is balanced, so no-trumps is attractive.
♠ 7 ♥ A 9 7 3 2 ♦ K Q 8 6 ♣ Q J 4	You opened 1♥. Your rebid after 2♥ or 1NT? Over 2♥, you should pass—no 26 points—but over 1NT, prefer a 2♦ rebid. Your hand is unbalanced and so a trump contract figures to be a better chance.
♠ A Q 8 6 4 ♥ A K 9 3 ♦ A Q ♣ J 7	You opened 1♠. Your rebid after 2♠ or 1NT? You have more than 20 points and therefore enough for game opposite your partner's 6–9 points. Over 2♠, bid 4♠. Over 1NT, force to game with a jump-shift to 3♥.
♠ 9 ♥ K Q 8 ♦ A K 8 7 4 3 ♣ A 9 3	You opened 1♦. Your rebid after 2♦ or 1NT? Game is possible but not certain. In both cases, rebid 3♦ to invite game. Responder will pass if minimum, but will bid again with a maximum (8–9 points).

AFTER A SUIT RESPONSE AT THE 1-LEVEL (E.G., 1♣ : 1♥, . . . ?)

(a) Opener has 12–15 points. With a minimum opening, opener makes a minimum rebid. You must not make a jump-rebid as opener unless you have a strong hand. In order of preference, opener's possible rebids are:

- **Raise responder's suit.** This requires 4-card support since the suit bid by responder need not have more than four cards in it. The only time opener would not raise responder's suit at once is if the bidding has started 1♣: 1♦ and opener has a 4-card major as well as support for diamonds. Show your major first rather than support your partner's minor.

- **Bid a new suit at the 1-level.** The new suit must have four cards in it, but any suit quality will do. Prefer to bid a new suit at the 1-level to rebidding 1NT or repeating your first suit.

- **Rebid 1NT if your hand is balanced.**

- **Bid a new suit at the 2-level lower than your first suit.** With a minimum opening, you should not rebid higher than two of your first suit unless you are supporting responder's suit.

- **Rebid your first suit as a last resort.** To rebid your suit after a 1-level response, the suit must have extra length (more than the opening promised).

(b) Opener has 16–18 points. In order of preference, opener should:

- **Jump-raise responder's suit to the 3-level.** Opener must have 4-card support for this. The only time opener would not raise responder at once is if the bidding has begun 1♣: 1♦, and opener has a 4-card major as well as support for diamonds. In that case, show the major first.

- **Bid a new suit at the 1-level or 2-level.**

- **As a last resort, jump to the 3-level in the suit opened, provided that you have at least six cards in that suit.**

(c) **Opener has 19 points or more.** In order of preference, opener should:

- **Jump to game in responder's suit.** This requires 4-card support. The only time opener would not support responder at once is if the bidding has begun 1♣: 1♦, and opener has a 4-card major as well as support for diamonds. In that case, opener would jump-shift to two of the major rather than support the diamonds yet. Majors come first.

- **Jump to 2NT, provided that your hand is balanced.** Opener's jump to 2NT (e.g., 1♣: 1♥, 2NT) is forcing to game.

- **Jump-shift (i.e., make a jump-bid in a new suit).** The jump-shift denies a balanced hand, but is forcing to game as it promises 19 points up.

- **As a last resort, if none of the above is available, jump to game in your first suit, provided you have a very powerful 6-card suit (it should contain at least four honors) or a strong 7-card suit.**

♠ Q 8 ♥ 4 2 ♦ A J 8 7 3 ♣ A Q J 6	You opened 1♦. Your rebid after 1♥ or 1♠? In either case you should rebid 2♣, showing your second suit and denying a balanced hand (no NT rebid). Further action will depend on responder's rebid.
♠ A K 3 ♥ A Q 4 ♦ A 9 8 ♣ Q 10 3 2	You opened 1♣. Your rebid after 1♦, 1♥, or 1♠? In each case, rebid with a jump to 2NT showing a balanced 18–20 points and forcing to game. Responder may bid 3NT, suggest a suit contract or aim for slam.
♠ A 7 3 2 ♥ 6 ♦ A Q J 9 5 ♣ K 8 3	You opened 1♦. Your rebid after 1♥ or 1♠? Over 1♥, rebid 1♠ and not 2♦. Show a major rather than rebid a longer minor. Over 1♠, you are worth 17 points (via the singleton) and so you should jump-raise to 3♠.

RESPONDER'S REBID WITH A WEAK RESPONDING HAND

If the opener has made a minimum rebid, confirming a hand in the 12–15 point range, responder is allowed to pass. However, responder is not obliged to pass if opener's rebid is unsuitable, but responder with a weak hand must not make a strong rebid. Responder is entitled to bid again with a weak hand, provided that responder's rebid is:

- **A raise of opener's second suit** (e.g., 1♣: 1♥, 1♠: 2♠). This still shows just 6–9 points in the same way that an immediate raise (1♠: 2♠) shows 6–9 points. Four trumps are needed to raise opener's second suit.

- **A preference to opener's first suit** (e.g., 1♦: 1♥, 1♠: 2♦). This also shows just 6–9 points in the same way that an immediate raise of opener's first suit (1♦: 2♦) shows 6–9 points.

- **A rebid of 1NT shows 6–9 points in the same way that an initial response of 1NT shows 6–9 points.**

- **As a last resort, you may rebid your own suit, provided that it contains at least six cards or is a very strong 5-card suit.**

If opener's rebid is a jump showing 16–18 points, the responder is permitted to pass with just 6–7 points, but is expected to bid on to game with 8+ points, since the partnership could then have 26 points or better.

If opener's rebid is a change of suit, opener may have up to 18 points (opener's range for a change of suit is 12–18 since 19 points or more are needed for a jump-shift rebid). Accordingly, responder strives to find a rebid with 8 points or better, since the partnership could have 26 points.

If opener's rebid is a jump, showing 18/19 points or more (a jump-shift or a jump to 2NT or a jump to game), responder is forced to bid again if game has not yet been reached, but is permitted to pass, of course, if opener's rebid is already a game (e.g., 1♥: 1♠, 4♥).

♠ A J 8 7 6   Your partner opened 1♦, you responded 1♠. Now
♥ 7 3 2   if your partner rebids 1NT, 2♦ or 2♠, you should
♦ K 5 4   pass but if your partner bids 2♣, you should rebid
♣ 8 6   2♦. Show a preference for one of your partner's suits
                 rather than rebid an ordinary 5-card suit.

♠ A 10 9 7 3 2   If your partner opened 1♦ and you responded
♥ Q 4   1♠, then if your partner rebids 1NT, 2♦ or 2♥,
♦ 2   you should rebid 2♠, showing long spades but a
♣ 8 7 5 3   minimum response (6–9 points), but if your partner
                 rebids 2NT or 3♠, you should rebid 4♠.

PARTNERSHIP BIDDING PRACTICE
FEATURING RESPONDING WITH WEAK HANDS

West is the dealer on each hand. How should the bidding go?

	WEST		EAST		WEST		EAST
9.	♠ K Q 7 4	9.	♠ 6 5	15.	♠ K 7 2	15.	♠ A J
	♥ A 8		♥ K J 5 2		♥ A 8 3		♥ K Q 9 7 2
	♦ 9 7 3		♦ A 8 6 4		♦ Q 9 5		♦ A J 6 2
	♣ A 7 6 2		♣ 8 4 3		♣ 9 6 5 3		♣ 8 7
10.	♠ A J 8	10.	♠ 4	16.	♠ A K J 7 2	16.	♠ 4 3
	♥ K Q 3		♥ J 10 8 6 5		♥ K Q J		♥ 9 6 5
	♦ A J 4		♦ K Q 5		♦ A 9		♦ K Q 7 4
	♣ K Q 7 2		♣ 8 6 4 3		♣ 8 6 4		♣ K J 10 5
11.	♠ 8 4 3	11.	♠ A 9 7 2	17.	♠ Q 10 5	17.	♠ A 8 4
	♥ A 6 2		♥ K Q 4		♥ Q J 6		♥ K 9 2
	♦ K 5		♦ A 8		♦ 8 2		♦ K Q 7 6 5
	♣ 10 9 7 6 2		♣ K Q J 3		♣ K 9 5 4 3		♣ 8 2
12.	♠ A Q 9 5	12.	♠ 6 3	18.	♠ A 8 6 3	18.	♠ 5 4
	♥ K Q 7 3		♥ J 6 5 2		♥ 8 4		♥ K Q 9 7
	♦ 8 6		♦ A K 4 3		♦ A 10 6 5		♦ K 7 4 2
	♣ K 7 2		♣ 9 8 5		♣ K Q 2		♣ 7 6 5
13.	♠ 9 7 6 4 2	13.	♠ A K 5 3	19.	♠ Q 8 3 2	19.	♠ J 9 7 4
	♥ 7 5		♥ A 9 3		♥ K Q 9 5		♥ 7 4 3
	♦ A 8 5 4		♦ 6		♦ 9 4		♦ A Q
	♣ J 9		♣ A K 8 4 3		♣ 8 4 3		♣ K Q J 6
14.	♠ A J 8 7 6	14.	♠ 5 2	20.	♠ A J 7 5	20.	♠ K 9 8 3
	♥ A K Q 3		♥ J 9 7 6		♥ 4		♥ 8 7 6 5 2
	♦ A J		♦ K 6 4 3		♦ K 4 3		♦ Q J 5
	♣ 7 6		♣ K 8 4		♣ A K Q 6 2		♣ 4

Play Hands on Weak Responding Hands

Hand 9: Drawing Trumps—Discarding a Loser on Dummy's Winner
Dealer North: Nil vulnerable

NORTH
♠ A K Q 9 8 3
♥ A 8 6
♦ Q 3
♣ J 10

WEST
♠ 10 2
♥ 4
♦ K 10 7 6
♣ 8 7 6 5 4 2

EAST
♠ J
♥ K Q J 10 5 3
♦ A 9 8 2
♣ 9 3

SOUTH
♠ 7 6 5 4
♥ 9 7 2
♦ J 5 4
♣ A K Q

WEST	NORTH	EAST	SOUTH
	1♠	2♥	2♠
Pass	3♠	Pass	4♠
Pass	Pass	Pass	

Bidding: North's 3♠ invites South to bid game with 8+ points.
Lead: ♥K, top of sequence.
Play: North wins ♥A, draws trumps in two rounds and plays A, K, Q of clubs to discard a red suit loser. It is normal to draw trumps first.
Wrong play: (1) Failing to win the ♥A at trick one. West would ruff the next heart and could defeat 4♠. (2) Playing clubs before drawing trumps. East ruffs the third round of clubs and 4♠ would be beaten.

Hand 10: Drawing Trumps—Setting Up Winners to Discard a Loser
Dealer East: N-S vulnerable

NORTH
♠ 10 6
♥ 8 2
♦ 9 8 4 3
♣ K 10 6 4 2

WEST
♠ K J 9 8
♥ 6 5 4
♦ J 5
♣ J 8 7 3

EAST
♠ A Q 4 3
♥ A K 7
♦ K Q 10 7 2
♣ 9

SOUTH
♠ 7 5 2
♥ Q J 10 9 3
♦ A 6
♣ A Q 5

WEST	NORTH	EAST	SOUTH
		1♦	1♥
1♠	Pass	4♠	All pass

Bidding: West is just worth the 1♠ response and East re-values to 21 points, counting 3 for the singleton since support is held for West's suit.
Lead: ♥8. Lead your partner's suit. From a doubleton, lead the top card.
Play: Win the ♥A. Draw trumps in three rounds. Next play the jack of diamonds to knock out the ace and so set up the other diamonds as winners. When the lead is regained, play the diamonds and discard a heart loser and two clubs. Set up a long suit before playing to ruff losers.

Hand 11: Ruffing a Loser in Dummy—Drawing Trumps Delayed

Dealer South: Both vulnerable

WEST	NORTH	EAST	SOUTH
			1♥
Pass	1NT	Pass	3♥
Pass	Pass	Pass	

NORTH
♠ 5 3
♥ 9 2
♦ K Q 9 3
♣ J 8 7 4 2

WEST
♠ Q J 10 8
♥ Q J 5
♦ 5 4 2
♣ K 6 3

EAST
♠ 7 6 4 2
♥ 10 7
♦ A J 10 8
♣ A 10 9

SOUTH
♠ A K 9
♥ A K 8 6 4 3
♦ 7 6
♣ Q 5

Bidding: South's 3♥ shows six hearts and 16-18 points, inviting North to bid game with more than 6–7 points.
Lead: ♠Q. Top of sequence.
Play: South should win and play the other spade winner, followed by the third spade, ruffed in dummy. Next, the A-K of hearts should be followed by a diamond to the king.
Wrong play: Failing to ruff the spade loser in dummy. If South plays A-K of hearts at once, dummy is unable to ruff a spade and there are five losers.

Hand 12: Urgent Discard of a Loser—Drawing Trumps Delayed

Dealer West: Nil vulnerable

WEST	NORTH	EAST	SOUTH
1♣	Pass	1♥	1♠
2NT	Pass	3♥	Pass
4♥	Pass	Pass	Pass

NORTH
♠ 5 4
♥ 8 6
♦ A 10 9 3 2
♣ 10 7 5 4

WEST
♠ A 9 8
♥ K 4 2
♦ Q J 8
♣ A K Q 3

EAST
♠ 7 3 2
♥ Q J 10 9 5
♦ K 7 6
♣ 6 2

SOUTH
♠ K Q J 10 6
♥ A 7 3
♦ 5 4
♣ J 9 8

Bidding: West, too strong to open 1NT, makes a jump-rebid in NT. East repeats the hearts to show five, asking West to choose 4♥ or 3NT.
Lead: ♠K. Top of sequence.
Play: Win ♠A. Play ♣A, ♣K, ♣Q to discard one spade loser. Then lead trumps. When the lead is regained, draw the missing trumps, followed by diamonds to knock out the ♦A. You lose one spade, one heart, and one diamond. Do not lead trumps before taking a discard on dummy's clubs. Do not lead the fourth round of clubs.

Chapter 5
Responding with Strong Hands

Responding to an Opening of 1♣, 1♦, 1♥ or 1♠

Hands with 10 or more high card points are considered strong hands for responder. Hands with exactly 10 HCP are border line. With 10 HCP and a 4-3-3-3 pattern, the 1NT response would be acceptable. Other patterns with exactly 10 HCP would be too strong for 1NT. Hands with 10 HCP and a 4-3-3-3 pattern would be acceptable for the weak raise of opener's suit to the 2-level as long as trump support is present. Other patterns with 10 HCP would be too strong.

Responder's most common action with a strong hand is to change suit, await further information from opener and then either make a decision as to the best contract or make another descriptive bid to help your partner. When responder is changing suit, the normal order of priorities applies:

- Bid your longest suit first.
- With 5-5 or 6-6 patterns, bid the higher-ranking suit first.
- 4-card suits are bid up-the-line.

Since responder has a strong hand, there will not be any need to bid the suits out of natural order. Responder might have to bid suits in a different order with a weak hand (see page 41). When bidding a new suit, responder may bid at the 1-level or at the 2-level. At the 1-level a new suit shows 6 points or more, while a new suit at the 2-level shows 10 points or more, provided that it is not a jump-shift. When bidding a new suit, responder will bid it at the cheapest possible level and a suit response at the 1-level does not deny a strong hand. If responder does jump-shift (e.g., 1♣: 2♥ *or* 1♠: 3♣), responder shows 19 points or more and usually a powerful 5-card or longer suit. The jump-shift is very rare. It is forcing to game and strongly suggests slam possibilities.

Aside from changing suit, responder has three specific strong responses, but the hand must fit the requirements before these bids are chosen:

- 2NT response—11–12 points, balanced, stoppers in unbid suits.
- 3NT response—13–15 points, balanced, stoppers in unbid suits.
- Jump-raise, e.g., 1♠: 3♠—10–12 points and 4+ trump support.

The 2NT and 3NT responses deny support for opener and deny a 4-card major. They are not common, but if the hand fits, prefer 2NT/3NT to bidding a minor. Minimum for a stopper is A-x, K-x, Q-x-x, or J-x-x-x.

Responder's general strategy of developing a strong hand:

10–12 points: If unsuitable for 2NT or a jump-raise, bid a new suit and then bid again, inviting game. For example, 1♠: 2♣, 2♦: 3♦ . . . *or* 1♠: 2♣, 2♦: 3♣ . . . *or* 1♥: 2♣, 2♦: 2♥ . . .

13–15 points: These hands are strong enough to bid to a game. If the hand fits 3NT, choose that response. If not, change suit and bid game on the next round if you know the best spot *or* change suit again, which will require the opener to bid once more *or* jump on the next round. For example, 1♦: 1♠, 1NT: 4♠ . . . *or* 1♥: 2♣, 2♥: 4♥ . . .

16–18 points: Start by changing suit. On the next round, either change suit again or decide whether to bid game or look for slam. If opener has confirmed a minimum opening, be content with game, but if opener has promised better than minimum, you should plan to look for a slam.

19 points or more: Jump-shift if possible. If not, change suit and judge which slam to try for after opener has told you more with the rebid.

An opening hand facing an opening hand should produce a game.

An opening hand facing an opener who jumps can produce a slam if a good trump fit is located. A 19-up hand opposite an opening will usually produce a slam if a good trump fit is located.

RESPONDING TO AN 1NT OPENING

With 10 points or more opposite an 1NT opening, game is a good bet. Jump directly to game if you know the best spot (e.g., 1NT: 3NT or 1NT: 4♠) or you may jump to 3-in-a-suit (e.g., 1NT: 3♥) which is forcing to game and shows a 5-card suit. Opener will support your suit if possible, but if opener holds only a doubleton, opener will rebid 3NT. You may also use the Stayman Convention (see page 127) with 8 points or more and a 4-card major. With 8 points or more, game is possible—make sure you do not respond to 1NT with a weak response of 2-in-a-suit, which shows only 0–7 points and asks opener to pass. When you have 8 or 9 points only and your long suit is a minor or you have both minor suits, the best bet is to stick with no-trumps.

If you have 16 points or more opposite an 1NT opening, you have slam prospects and this is covered in more detail in Chapter 8.

♠ A Q 8 6 4 ♥ A K 9 5 ♦ 7 3 2 ♣ 5	Suppose your partner opens 1♣. You know you have enough for a game, but which game? As you cannot tell, respond 1♠ and await opener's rebid. Over 2♠, bid 4♠ but over 2♣, bid 2♥, a new suit, and forcing. Over 1NT, jump to 3♥, forcing.
♠ A Q 8 6 4 2 ♥ A K J ♦ 7 3 2 ♣ 5	If your partner opens 1♣, respond 1♠. Then over 2♠, rebid 4♠. Over 1NT, rebid 4♠ as opener figures to have 2-3 spades. The 1NT rebid by opener is normally balanced. Over 2♣, choose a 3♠ rebid, showing a strong hand with six spades.

♠ A 9 5
♥ Q J 6
♦ K J 8
♣ Q J 9 4

If your partner opens the bidding, you have enough for a game, no matter which opening bid was made. Over any suit opening, you are worth 3NT, showing 13-15 points and a balanced hand. It is useful to restrict the 3NT response to a 4-3-3-3 pattern.

♠ 8
♥ A 9 8 5 4
♦ A Q 7 4 3
♣ J 2

If your partner opens the bidding 1♠, respond 2♥, the higher suit with a 5-5 pattern. Normally, responder's change of suit promises no more than a 4-card suit. However, 1♠: 2♥ *is an exception and promises five hearts or more.*

♠ A 7 5 2
♥ 5
♦ A J 6 3
♣ A Q 9 4

If your partner opens 1♥, respond 1♠. 4-card suits are bid up-the-line whether opening or responding. "Cheapest" suit does not mean "lowest" suit. 1♠ is cheaper than 2♣. It would be an error to respond 3NT, since that guarantees a balanced hand.

♠ A J 8
♥ Q J 6 4
♦ 5 4
♣ K 9 8 3

Hands of 11–12 points often start with a change of suit. Over a 1♣ opening, respond 1♥ and do the same over a 1♦ opening. Over 1♥, respond 3♥ to show 10–12 points and 4-card support. After an 1♠ opening, respond 2♣, bidding up-the-line.

♠ A K Q J 7 4
♥ A K 8
♦ 8 7
♣ Q 2

If your partner opens the bidding with 1♣, 1♦, or 1♥, you should respond 2♠, a jump-shift showing 19 points or more. This is forcing to game and strongly suggests a slam is possible. The jump-shift normally shows a strong 5-card or longer suit.

♠ 8 5
♥ A Q 4 2
♦ A 8 7
♣ K J 5 4

If your partner opens 1♠, bid 2♣, "up-the-line." You have the values for 3NT, but restrict that reply to a 4-3-3-3 hand with the 4-card suit a minor. Over 1♥, bid 2♣, intending to jump to 4♥ on the next round. Over 1♣ or 1♦, respond 1♥.

EXERCISES ON RESPONDING WITH A STRONG HAND

A. Your partner opens 1♣, next player passes. What is your response?

1.	♠ K Q 8	2.	♠ K Q 8	3.	♠ 8 7 4	4.	♠ K Q 8
	♥ A J 7		♥ A J 7		♥ A J 7		♥ A J 7 4 2
	♦ K 9 7 2		♦ K 9 7 2		♦ K 9 7 2		♦ K 9
	♣ 8 4 3		♣ A 8 4		♣ A Q 3		♣ J 8 3

5.	♠ A J 8 2	6.	♠ A J 8 2	7.	♠ A J 8 2	8.	♠ 7 6
	♥ A J 7 6		♥ A J 7 6		♥ 7			♥ A Q J 4
	♦ A Q 7 4		♦ 7			♦ A Q 7 4		♦ A K 9
	♣ 7			♣ A Q 7 4		♣ A J 7 6		♣ A Q 3 2

B. Your partner opens 1♦, next player passes. What is your response?

1.	♠ A 7	2.	♠ A 7	3.	♠ A Q 8 4	4.	♠ A Q 8 4 3
	♥ A 9 7		♥ A 9 7 2		♥ K Q 7 2		♥ K Q 7 3 2
	♦ Q J 8 4 3		♦ Q J 8 4 3		♦ K 3		♦ K 3
	♣ 9 6 4		♣ K 6			♣ 7 6 5		♣ 5

C. Your partner opens 1♥, next player passes. What is your response?

1.	♠ 8 4	2.	♠ A Q 9 8	3.	♠ 8 4 3	4.	♠ 8 4
	♥ K Q 7 2		♥ K 7 2		♥ K 3		♥ 3
	♦ A J 8 5		♦ Q 4 3 2		♦ Q J 7 6		♦ A Q 9 7 6
	♣ 8 6 3		♣ 7 6		♣ A J 9 8		♣ A K 8 4 3

D. Your partner opens 1♠, next player passes. What is your response?

1.	♠ A J 7	2.	♠ A J 7	3.	♠ 7 4	4.	♠ Q 8 4 3
	♥ 6 4 2		♥ K Q 9 3 2		♥ A Q 8 6		♥ K 8
	♦ K Q 9 3		♦ K 7		♦ A K 9 3		♦ A J 6 3
	♣ J 8 7		♣ 8 4 2		♣ 8 4 2		♣ K 6 2

E. Your partner opens 1NT, next player passes. What is your response?

1.	♠ K Q 8 7 6	2.	♠ A 7	3.	♠ - - -	4.	♠ 4
	♥ A 8			♥ K 8 3		♥ J 9 8 7 6 3		♥ K Q 9 5 3
	♦ J 6 3 2			♦ J 9 8 7 3 2		♦ A K 3 2		♦ A Q 7 6 4
	♣ J 8			♣ Q 6		♣ J 6 5		♣ A 3

Opener's Rebids after a Strong Response

After a Suit Response at the 1-level

A suit response at the 1-level can be a weak responding hand or a strong responding hand. Opener's rebids have been discussed on pages 45–48.

After a Response of 2NT or 3NT or a Jump-raise

With a minimum opening, opener should pass—but with extra values—bid to game opposite 2NT and consider slam after 3NT if you have a powerful opening. Slam bidding is covered in Chapter 8. Where the response was 2NT or 3NT, opener will stay with no-trumps with a balanced hand, but will try to play in a trump contract if the hand is unbalanced. For example, after 1♠: 2NT, opener could rebid 3♥ to show five spades and four hearts and a desire to play in one of the majors rather than no-trumps.

After a Jump-shift Response

Opener should support responder's suit with three or more trumps. Without support, make a natural rebid, bidding a second suit if possible.

After a Suit Response at the 2-level (e.g., 1♥: 2♣)

With a minimum opening, your order of priorities is:

- Support responder to the 3-level (e.g., 1♥: 2♣, 3♣). Opener would choose not to support responder at once only after 1♠: 2♣ or 1♠: 2♦, where opener with four hearts would rather bid 2♥ to show the other major.
- Bid a new suit lower-ranking than the first suit (e.g., 1♥: 2♣, 2♦).
- Repeat the first suit with no other convenient bid (e.g., 1♥: 2♣, 2♥).

The suit need not be more than five cards long. The rebid of opener's first suit is used to confirm, a minimum opening with no cheaper suit to bid.

- Rebid 2NT with a minimum balanced hand. A jump-rebid to 3NT after a 2-level response shows 18–20 points and a balanced hand.

Opener's change of suit to a lower suit (e.g., 1♠: 2♦, 2♥) = 12–18 points (a jump-shift = 19 points or more). It can be a minimum opening or a strong hand and so change-of-suit after a 2-level response is forcing.

A new suit by opener beyond 2-in-the-suit-opened (e.g., 1♦: 2♣, 2♥) shows better than a minimum opening, say 16 points or more. Logically it is forcing to game since responder has 10 points or more for the 2-level response and opener has shown 16 points or more with for a strong rebid.

EXERCISES ON REBIDS AFTER A STRONG RESPONSE

A. West 1♦: East 2NT. West's rebid?

1.	♠ K 7	2.	♠ 7 5	3.	♠ 6	4.	♠ A 7 2
	♥ A K 3		♥ K Q 4 3		♥ 5 4		♥ 6 5 3
	♦ A 9 6 5		♦ A K J 6 2		♦ A K J 8 6		♦ K Q 7 6
	♣ A J 5 2		♣ Q 4		♣ A Q J 6 3		♣ A 4 3

B. West 1♦: East 2♣. West's rebid?

1.	♠ K Q 3	2.	♠ K Q 3	3.	♠ K 3 2	4.	♠ 7 2
	♥ A 8 7		♥ A 8 7		♥ A Q 8 6		♥ A 2
	♦ K J 7 4		♦ K Q J 4		♦ K J 9 8 7		♦ A Q 8 7 4
	♣ 8 6 2		♣ A 10 7		♣ 4		♣ K 4 3 2

C. West 1♥: East 2♣. West's rebid?

1.	♠ A 4	2.	♠ A 9 8 3	3.	♠ 9 7 5	4.	♠ Q 8
	♥ K Q 7 6 2		♥ K Q 7 6 2		♥ A K J 7 3		♥ A J 9 7 4 2
	♦ A 9 8 3		♦ 7 6		♦ 9 7 2		♦ K Q 5
	♣ 7 6		♣ A 4		♣ A 10		♣ J 8

5.	♠ A J 8	6.	♠ A J 8	7.	♠ A J 8 2	8.	♠ 7 2
	♥ A Q 7 6 4		♥ A Q 6 3 2		♥ A Q J 9 4 2		♥ A 9 7 3 2
	♦ Q 7 4		♦ K Q 4		♦ A 4		♦ A K Q 5
	♣ 9 2		♣ K 2		♣ 3		♣ A 8

D. West 1♥: East 2NT. West's rebid?

1.	♠ A K 7 4	2.	♠ A J 7	3.	♠ A 6	4.	♠ - - -
	♥ K J 9 5 4		♥ K J 9 8 4 3		♥ A 9 7 5 3		♥ A Q 8 7 5
	♦ 7		♦ 7		♦ K Q J		♦ K Q 7 6 3
	♣ A 4 3		♣ K Q 2		♣ 7 6 2		♣ Q J 8

E. West 1♠: East 2♦. West's rebid?

1.	♠ A K 9 8 3	2.	♠ A K 9 8 3	3.	♠ A K 8 7 3 2	4.	♠ A Q J 9 8 6 2
	♥ K Q 7 6		♥ 8 5 3		♥ A J 3		♥ 7 2
	♦ 4		♦ 4		♦ 9 2		♦ K Q J
	♣ 8 5 3		♣ K Q 7 6		♣ K Q		♣ J

PARTNERSHIP BIDDING PRACTICE
FEATURING RESPONDING WITH STRONG HANDS

West is the dealer on each hand. How should the bidding go?

	WEST		EAST		WEST		EAST
21.	♠ A J 9 7 ♥ K 9 4 ♦ 7 6 ♣ A J 3 2	21.	♠ 8 2 ♥ A Q 7 2 ♦ K 9 4 3 ♣ K Q 6	27.	♠ A J 8 ♥ K Q 7 ♦ K 9 4 2 ♣ 7 6 2	27.	♠ K 7 2 ♥ 9 5 ♦ 8 5 3 ♣ A K 8 4 3
22.	♠ A Q J 7 3 ♥ 4 ♦ 7 ♣ A J 9 5 4 3	22.	♠ 8 2 ♥ A Q 7 2 ♦ K 9 4 3 ♣ K Q 6	28.	♠ A 7 ♥ 7 2 ♦ K Q J 5 3 ♣ A Q 10 6	28.	♠ 9 4 3 ♥ K J 8 4 ♦ A 7 ♣ K 5 3 2
23.	♠ A K J ♥ K 7 ♦ 7 2 ♣ A J 9 8 4 3	23.	♠ 9 5 ♥ Q 10 6 5 2 ♦ A K J 9 ♣ 6 2	29.	♠ A 10 6 ♥ K 8 4 3 ♦ K Q 9 6 2 ♣ 8	29.	♠ K 5 ♥ Q J 6 5 ♦ 8 7 ♣ A K 9 4 3
24.	♠ J 6 ♥ K J 3 ♦ Q 7 ♣ A J 9 8 4 3	24.	♠ 9 5 ♥ Q 10 6 5 2 ♦ A K J 9 ♣ K 2	30.	♠ A 6 ♥ 4 3 ♦ A Q 8 7 4 ♣ K Q J 3	30.	♠ 7 2 ♥ K Q J 8 5 2 ♦ J 6 ♣ A 5 2
25.	♠ 7 6 4 3 ♥ A Q 8 7 ♦ 6 ♣ A K 4 3	25.	♠ A J 9 2 ♥ 4 2 ♦ A K 9 7 5 ♣ 8 6	31.	♠ K Q 6 ♥ 7 2 ♦ A Q 9 7 5 3 ♣ J 8	31.	♠ A 8 4 3 ♥ A 10 5 3 ♦ K 4 ♣ K 9 2
26.	♠ Q J 3 ♥ A Q 8 7 ♦ 6 ♣ A K 5 4 3	26.	♠ K 4 ♥ 6 2 ♦ A K J 8 7 5 ♣ 9 7 2	32.	♠ 7 ♥ J 2 ♦ A J 7 6 2 ♣ A Q 9 7 5	32.	♠ A K 8 4 3 ♥ K Q 9 4 ♦ 5 3 ♣ J 6

PARTNERSHIP BIDDING PRACTICE
FEATURING RESPONDING WITH STRONG HANDS

West is the dealer on each hand. How should the bidding go?

WEST	EAST	WEST	EAST
33. ♠ 8 6 5 ♥ A Q 7 4 3 2 ♦ A K 9 ♣ 2	33. ♠ A K 9 4 2 ♥ 6 ♦ Q 8 3 ♣ Q J 10 5	39. ♠ A K J 8 7 ♥ A Q J 6 3 ♦ 7 3 ♣ 8	39. ♠ 6 5 4 ♥ 8 2 ♦ A K 8 6 2 ♣ K 7 2
34. ♠ 8 ♥ A Q 7 4 3 2 ♦ A K 9 ♣ 8 6 2	34. ♠ A K 9 4 2 ♥ 6 ♦ Q 8 3 ♣ Q J 10 5	40. ♠ A K J 8 7 ♥ A Q J 6 3 ♦ 7 3 ♣ 8	40. ♠ 6 ♥ K 8 4 ♦ A Q 8 6 4 ♣ Q 9 7 2
35. ♠ A J 9 ♥ K Q 8 4 3 ♦ A Q 4 2 ♣ 6	35. ♠ Q 8 2 ♥ J 5 ♦ J 8 7 ♣ A K 8 7 3	41. ♠ A K J 8 7 ♥ A Q J 6 ♦ 7 3 ♣ 8 5	41. ♠ 9 6 ♥ K 8 ♦ A Q 8 6 4 ♣ Q 9 7 2
36. ♠ K 9 5 2 ♥ A K J 8 7 ♦ Q 3 2 ♣ K	36. ♠ 8 6 3 ♥ Q ♦ A 6 5 ♣ A Q 8 6 5 2	42. ♠ K Q 6 5 4 ♥ A 2 ♦ A Q 9 8 3 ♣ Q	42. ♠ 8 ♥ K Q 8 7 6 3 ♦ K J 6 ♣ J 7 2
37. ♠ A K J 2 ♥ K 9 7 6 4 ♦ J 2 ♣ 6 3	37. ♠ Q 7 6 5 4 ♥ 5 3 ♦ A K 9 4 3 ♣ 4	43. ♠ A Q 8 7 4 ♥ 6 5 ♦ K Q J ♣ 9 8 3	43. ♠ J 6 ♥ A 8 7 4 3 ♦ A 9 5 ♣ J 4 2
38. ♠ 6 ♥ A Q J 7 6 ♦ K Q J 5 ♣ 9 3 2	38. ♠ Q 8 7 ♥ 8 3 2 ♦ A 9 8 3 2 ♣ A J	44. ♠ A Q 8 7 4 ♥ J 6 2 ♦ K Q J ♣ 9 8	44. ♠ J 6 ♥ A K 8 4 3 ♦ A 9 5 ♣ J 6 4

Play Hands on Strong Responding Hands

Hand 13: Coping with a Bad Break—The Marked Finesse

Dealer North: Both vulnerable

WEST	NORTH	EAST	SOUTH
	1♣	Pass	1♥
1♠	2♥	Pass	4♥
Pass	Pass	Pass	

NORTH
♠ 10 7 4
♥ A K Q 10
♦ K
♣ J 8 7 6 2

WEST
♠ A K 8 6 3
♥ J 9 8 2
♦ A 9
♣ Q 9

EAST
♠ 9 5 2
♥ - - -
♦ 10 8 7 6 5 4
♣ 10 5 4 3

SOUTH
♠ Q J
♥ 7 6 5 4 3
♦ Q J 3 2
♣ A K

Bidding: With 13 points opposite an opening, South always intended to reach game. When North raised hearts that settled the matter.

Lead: ♠A, normal from A-K suits.

Play: After the top spades and the ♦A, South wins the next trick and plays the ♥A. When East shows out, play a club to hand and lead a heart towards dummy, *finessing* the 10 when West plays low. Draw West's trumps and use the ♠10 or the ♣J to discard a diamond loser.

Hand 14: Drawing Trumps—The Marked Finesse

Dealer East: Nil vulnerable

WEST	NORTH	EAST	SOUTH
		1♠	Pass
3♠	Pass	4♠	All pass

NORTH
♠ - - -
♥ 10 8 5 4
♦ A 7 5 3
♣ 8 7 4 3 2

WEST
♠ A K J 5
♥ J 7 3 2
♦ J 9 4
♣ J 6

EAST
♠ 9 7 6 4 3 2
♥ A K Q
♦ K Q
♣ Q 9

SOUTH
♠ Q 10 8
♥ 9 6
♦ 10 8 6 2
♣ A K 10 5

Bidding: West's 3♠ jump-raise shows 10–12 points and 4+ trumps. It invites game. With extras, East accepts.

Lead: ♣A, normal from A-K suits.

Play: South cashes the top clubs and shifts to a red suit. When East comes in, East leads a spade to the ace. North shows out, East knows that South began with Q-10-8 and still has Q-x left. To capture the queen, East returns to hand with a heart and leads a spade, finessing dummy's jack. The last trump is drawn and East loses at most one diamond and two clubs.

Hand 15: Drawing Trumps in the Correct Order—The Marked Finesse
Dealer South: Both vulnerable

NORTH
♠ A 9 7 5
♥ K Q 4 2
♦ 8 5 2
♣ K Q

WEST
♠ Q J 4
♥ 9
♦ A K Q 10 7
♣ 8 6 4 2

EAST
♠ 10 8 6 3 2
♥ J 8 6 5
♦ 9 4
♣ 7 5

SOUTH
♠ K
♥ A 10 7 3
♦ J 6 3
♣ A J 10 9 3

WEST	NORTH	EAST	SOUTH
			1♣
1♦	1♥	Pass	2♥
Pass	4♥	All pass	

Bidding: 1♥ was "up-the-line."

Lead: ♦9. Your partner's suit is first choice. Play high-low with a doubleton.

Play: After three diamond tricks and a black suit exit, play off the K-Q of hearts first (keep the A-10 tenace intact). When West discards, finesse against East's jack, thus not losing a heart trick. If trumps were 3-2, the order of playing the top trumps would not matter. K-Q first caters for East holding J-x-x-x. Had West continued with a fourth diamond, North should ruff this in hand, not in dummy. If East over-ruffs, dummy can over-ruff.

Hand 16: Drawing Trumps—Marked Finesse—Repeating the Finesse
Dealer West: Nil vulnerable

NORTH
♠ - - -
♥ 10 9 6 3 2
♦ 9 7 5 4 2
♣ A K 8

WEST
♠ A J 10 7 4 3
♥ K 8 4
♦ J 10
♣ 6 3

EAST
♠ K 5 2
♥ Q J 7
♦ A K Q
♣ J 9 4 2

SOUTH
♠ Q 9 8 6
♥ A 5
♦ 8 6 3
♣ Q 10 7 5

WEST	NORTH	EAST	SOUTH
Pass	Pass	1NT	Pass
4♠	Pass	Pass	Pass

Bidding: After 1NT, West re-values to 11 points for a spade contract, enough for game opposite 15–17 points.

Lead: ♣A, normal from A-K suits.

Play: South plays the ♣7 on the ace and the ♣5 on the king. High-low on your partner's lead is a signal for your partner to continue that suit. West ruffs the next club and leads a spade to the king, high card from shortage first. When North shows out, West continues by finessing the jack of spades, leading a diamond to dummy and finessing the ♠10. The ♠A draws South's queen and West then sets up the heart winners.

Chapter 6
Bidding by a Passed Hand

Once you have passed initially, some of your bids have a different meaning as you cannot hold 13 points, otherwise you would have opened. Your weak responses are not affected: a raise of opener's suit to the two-level is still 6–9 points and the 1NT response is also still 6–9 points. A change of suit at the one-level now has a range of 6–12 points, as opposed to the wide-ranging 6+ points for a new suit response at the one-level by an unpassed hand.

Since a passed hand cannot hold 13 points, any jump-response shows exactly 10–11 points or a poor 12. Specifically:

- The jump to 2NT by a passed hand (e.g., Pass: 1♥, 2NT) is normal, a balanced hand, 10–12 points, and denies support for opener's suit.

- The jump-raise by a passed hand (e.g., Pass: 1♠, 3♠) is normal and shows 10–12 points and support for opener's suit.

- The jump-shift by a passed hand (e.g., Pass: 1♦, 2♠) shows 10–12 points and a strong 5-card suit. If the suit is only four cards long or if the suit is not strong, bid the suit at the cheapest level without a jump.

The most important rule about bidding by a passed hand is this:

A BID BY A PASSED HAND IS NOT FORCING.

This applies whether it is a jump bid or a change of suit so that the normal rules about change-of-suit forcing or jump-responses forcing to game do not apply when the responder is a passed hand. Because any bid by a passed hand is not forcing, it is vital to make a response which gives your partner the most important message in one bid. There might be no second chance. Therefore, raise a major suit as first priority. Do not bid a new suit when you have a major-suit raise available.

The change of suit to the 2-level still requires 10 points, but the range is 10–12 points rather than the normal 10 points or more. The 2-over-1 response by a passed hand usually shows a 5+ suit (since it may be passed by opener). With only 4-card suits, bid a suit at the 1-level if possible, as this does not show more than four cards, or respond 1NT or 2NT.

EXERCISES ON PASSED HAND BIDDING

A. You passed as dealer and your partner opens 1♣. What is your response?

1.	♠ K Q 6	2.	♠ A J	3.	♠ A Q J 4 3	4.	♠ K 8
	♥ K J 8		♥ K Q 3 2		♥ K 9		♥ A Q 9
	♦ Q 6 5 2		♦ J 7 6		♦ 7 6 5		♦ 6 3
	♣ J 9 4		♣ 8 7 4 2		♣ J 9 2		♣ J 9 8 5 3 2

B. You passed as dealer and your partner opens 1♥. What is your response?

1.	♠ A J	2.	♠ A J 8 4 2	3.	♠ K Q 6	4.	♠ A Q J 9 8
	♥ K 9 7 6		♥ Q 7 6 2		♥ 4 3		♥ J 6
	♦ 6 5 4		♦ 4 3		♦ J 10 4 3		♦ K 4 3
	♣ Q J 9 4		♣ 6 2		♣ A J 10 2		♣ 7 6 2

5.	♠ A 9 8 6	6.	♠ A 5 2	7.	♠ A 5 2	8.	♠ 5 2
	♥ 7		♥ 4 3		♥ 4		♥ 7 6 4 3
	♦ Q 9 8 4		♦ K J 9 8 2		♦ K J 8 2		♦ A K J 8
	♣ K J 8 2		♣ Q 4 2		♣ 9 7 5 4 3		♣ Q J 2

PARTNERSHIP BIDDING PRACTICE

West is the dealer on each hand. How should the bidding go?

	WEST		EAST		WEST		EAST
45.	♠ A J 7	45.	♠ 9 5	48.	♠ A 7 6 4 2	48.	♠ J 9 8
	♥ K 9 8 4		♥ A Q 6 3 2		♥ K J		♥ Q 4 3
	♦ 7 6 4 3 2		♦ A K 8		♦ Q 9 8		♦ 6 5 2
	♣ 6		♣ J 7 4		♣ J 6 2		♣ A K Q 9
46.	♠ A Q 7 2	46.	♠ K 9 4 3	49.	♠ A J 7	49.	♠ Q 3 2
	♥ K 9 8 3		♥ 7		♥ 8 7		♥ A 10 6
	♦ J 8 7		♦ A K 3		♦ K 8 2		♦ A 7 5
	♣ 4 2		♣ A J 9 5 3		♣ K 8 6 4 3		♣ A 9 7 2
47.	♠ Q 7	47.	♠ K 9 8 5 2	50.	♠ 7	50.	♠ Q J 6 4 3
	♥ A 8		♥ K 7 6		♥ A 9 8 2		♥ Q 7
	♦ Q J 8 6 4 3		♦ 9 5 2		♦ J 9 7 3		♦ A 8 5
	♣ 7 6 2		♣ A Q		♣ A Q 7 6		♣ K 5 2

Chapter 7

Super-strong Opening Bids

Hands with more than 21 HCP are too strong to open with a one-opening, since your partner will normally pass with 5 points or less.

♠ A K J 8 4 3 ♥ A K 3 ♦ A K Q ♣ 5	If you were to open this hand 1♠, imagine your dismay if the bidding went: Pass, Pass, Pass. With just two or three points, your partner would be right to pass, but game may be a great chance opposite even less.

To cope with such a powerhouse, open with a Two-Bid. The bid chosen depends on shape but if the hand is not balanced follow the normal rules: longest suit first; with a 5-5 or 6-6, bid the higher-ranking first; with 4-card suits only, bid up-the-line. Two specific openings cater for balanced hands:

- **2NT = 21–22 points and balanced shape.** Your partner is permitted to pass this with 0–3 points, but with any hope for game, your partner will respond. With a balanced hand, responder keeps to no-trumps, while with unbalanced shapes, bid three-in-a-suit (promises a 5-card suit) or bid game in a major suit with six cards or more in the major. The Stayman 3♣ Convention is also commonly used (see page 127).
- With 23+ points and a balanced hand, open 2♣. If your partner bids 2♦, negative, rebid 2NT with 23–24 points and 3NT with 25–28.

With a hand that is not balanced, open 2-in-a-suit on any hand with 22+ HCP or with fewer than 22 HCP if it is stronger than nine playing tricks.

How to Count Playing Tricks: *In your long suits (four or more cards):* Count the ace and king as winners. Count the queen as a winner if the suit contains another honor. Count every card after the third card as a winner. *In your short suits:* Count A = 1, K with another honor = 1, K with one or more cards but no other honor = ½, Q or J with at least one higher honor = ½ (but A-K-Q is, of course, three tricks). For example:

♠ A K Q 8 7 6 3 ♥ A K 5 ♦ A 3 ♣ 6	This hand is worth ten tricks with spades as trumps. It would be a tragedy to open 1♠ and be left there. Open 2♠ and insist on game. To open 4♠ has a different meaning—see Chapter 9.

Responding to a 2-Opening

While responder is expected to pass a one-opening with 0–5 points, *responder must reply to a two-opening*, no matter how weak the hand. **The two-in-a-suit opening is normally forcing to game.** This means that both partners must keep bidding until at least game is reached.

The negative reply to 2♣ is 2♦. To 2♦, 2♥, 2♠ it is 2NT.

The negative reply (0–7 points, any shape) is purely artificial because the responder has to bid. It need not be a balanced hand at all. If there happens to be an intervening bid over your partner's 2-opening, responder would pass to show the negative reply. There is no obligation to bid over an intervening bid, since opener has another chance to bid anyway.

Any other response shows a stronger hand, about 8 points or more, about one-and-one-half tricks or better. With a positive response, which often leads to a slam, responder should show support for opener's major suit opening as first priority. Other than the 2♣ opening, the first suit by a 2-opener should be a 5-card or longer suit and you may therefore support it with just three trumps. If opener repeats the first suit, responder may support it with a doubleton. To support opener's second suit requires four trumps, however, since the second suit need not have more than four cards. Where responder has a positive reply but lacks support for opener, the normal rules apply for bidding a new suit (longest first; with 5-5 or 6-6 patterns, bid the higher suit first; 4-card suits up-the-line). With a balanced hand without support for opener, responder may bid 3NT with about 8–10 high card points. Opener will not pass since slam is likely.

Rebids by the Opener

(a) After a 2NT response

Opener will bid a second suit of four or more cards as first choice. With no second suit to show, opener will rebid the first suit with six or more cards or rebid 3NT with a 5-3-3-2 pattern. Responder will strive to support opener. If that is not possible, responder may introduce a long suit or rebid 3NT. Responder will not pass the bidding out below game.

(b) After a positive response

Opener will support responder's suit if possible. If not, bid a second suit or rebid the first suit with six or more cards in it. Slam is highly likely after a positive response, but it is important to reach agreement on a trump suit first if possible. Slam bidding is covered in Chapter 8.

EXERCISES ON SUPER-STRONG OPENING BIDS

A. What is your opening bid on these hands?

1. ♠ A 6	2. ♠ A	3. ♠ A K Q 8 4	4. ♠ Q 7 5 4 3
♥ A K J 10 6 2	♥ A K Q	♥ A K J 9 8 7	♥ A K 6 5
♦ A Q	♦ A K J 10 6 5 2	♦ A	♦ A K
♣ K 8 3	♣ 5 3	♣ 4	♣ A 2

5. ♠ - - -	6. ♠ A K Q J
♥ A K Q 8 6 5 4	♥ A Q J 7
♦ A Q J 8 7 3	♦ 4
♣ - - -	♣ A K Q 8

B. Your partner opens 2♥, next player passes. What is your response?

1. ♠ 7 5 4	2. ♠ K 8 7	3. ♠ A 8 7	4. ♠ A 8 7
♥ 6 4 2	♥ 6 4	♥ 6 4	♥ 4 2
♦ 5 4 3 2	♦ K 6 5 3	♦ Q J 7 6	♦ K Q 5 3 2
♣ 7 6 3	♣ 9 8 6 4	♣ Q 9 6 2	♣ 9 8 4

5. ♠ A 8 7	6. ♠ A K 8 4	7. ♠ 7 6	8. ♠ A 7 6 2
♥ Q 9 8	♥ 8 7 5 3	♥ Q J 7 5	♥ 2
♦ K 7 4 3 2	♦ 4 2	♦ Q 8 7 6	♦ A J 7 5
♣ J 2	♣ K 8 6	♣ 8 5 4	♣ 9 8 5 2

C. West 2♠: East 2NT. West's rebid?

1. ♠ A K Q J 7	2. ♠ A K Q J 8 7 6	3. ♠ A Q 9 8 6 2
♥ A K J 4	♥ 5 3	♥ A K
♦ 4 3	♦ A 4	♦ A Q J
♣ A K	♣ A K	♣ A 5

4. ♠ A K Q 8 6	5. ♠ A Q J 9 8 6 5	6. ♠ A K Q J 7
♥ A Q 5	♥ A K Q J 8 3	♥ A
♦ A K 7	♦ - - -	♦ 7 4
♣ A 3	♣ - - -	♣ A K Q 6 3

D. West 2♠: East 2NT, West rebids 3♥. What should East rebid?

1. ♠ 6 5	2. ♠ 9 8 7	3. ♠ Q 8 7	4. ♠ 8
♥ 4 3	♥ 7 6	♥ 4	♥ 7 2
♦ Q J 6 5	♦ Q J 7 6 3	♦ 8 7 5 3 2	♦ A J 8 6 5 3 2
♣ J 8 7 6 4	♣ 4 3 2	♣ K 9 6 5	♣ 5 3 2

5. ♠ 6 5	6. ♠ J 8 7	7. ♠ 3 2	8. ♠ K 8
♥ 7 6 4 3	♥ Q 5 2	♥ 9	♥ Q 9 4 3
♦ 9 6 5 2	♦ 6 5 4 2	♦ Q J 8 7 6	♦ 6 3 2
♣ 9 8 3	♣ 5 3 2	♣ Q 10 9 4 2	♣ 7 5 3 2

E. West 2♥: East 2NT, West rebids 6♦. What should East call now?

1. ♠ J 7 6 5 4	2. ♠ 6 4 3 2	3. ♠ 8 6 5 3	4. ♠ 9 8 2
♥ 9 8 6	♥ 4 3	♥ 4	♥ A 7 6
♦ 5 4	♦ 8 7 5	♦ K 7 5	♦ 4 3
♣ 6 4 2	♣ 5 4 3 2	♣ 9 6 5 3 2	♣ 7 6 5 3 2

Partnership Bidding Practice

West is the dealer on each hand. How should the bidding go?

	WEST		EAST		WEST		EAST
51.	♠ A K Q 9	51.	♠ 6 4 3	54.	♠ 7	54.	♠ K J 9 8 5
	♥ Q 9		♥ J 10 8 5		♥ A K 2		♥ 6 3
	♦ A Q J 10 8 5		♦ 4 3 2		♦ K Q J 9 8 6 4		♦ 2
	♣ A		♣ K 6 3		♣ A K		♣ 10 9 7 6 4
52.	♠ Q 10 7	52.	♠ A K 8 6 3	55.	♠ 9 3	55.	♠ A K Q J 5
	♥ J 10 7 4		♥ K		♥ J 8 7 4		♥ A K 6 2
	♦ K 8 3 2		♦ - - -		♦ 6 3		♦ A K
	♣ 7 2		♣ A Q J 9 8 5 4		♣ Q 7 6 4 3		♣ K 2
53.	♠ A K J 9 8 7 3	53.	♠ 6 5 4	56.	♠ J 5 4	56.	♠ A 9
	♥ A 6 2		♥ J 10 4		♥ 9 7		♥ A Q 3
	♦ - - -		♦ Q 5 2		♦ Q 8 6 3		♦ A K 5 2
	♣ A K J		♣ 8 6 3 2		♣ J 7 4 3		♣ K Q 8 6

PLAY HANDS ON SUPER-STRONG OPENINGS

Hand 17: 2NT Opening—Suit Contract—Finessing

Dealer North: Nil vulnerable

WEST	NORTH	EAST	SOUTH
	2NT	Pass	4♥
Pass	Pass		

NORTH
♠ A Q J 3
♥ A K
♦ A J 4 2
♣ Q J 9

WEST
♠ K 10 9
♥ 10
♦ 8 6 5 3
♣ A K 7 4 2

EAST
♠ 7 5 4
♥ 9 5 4 2
♦ K Q 10 9
♣ 10 3

SOUTH
♠ 8 6 2
♥ Q J 8 7 6 3
♦ 7
♣ 8 6 5

Bidding: South knows that N-S must have eight or more hearts and has enough to bid game. Note that 3NT fails as there is no entry to the South hand.

Lead: ♣A, normal from A-K suits.

Play: East signals high-low, ♣10 then ♣3, and ruffs the third round. The ♦A wins the ♦K exit and the ♥A, ♥K are cashed. A diamond is ruffed and the last trump is drawn. A spade is led: low–queen—low. When this finesse works, ruff another diamond and finesse the jack of spades for ten tricks.

Hand 18: Demand Opening—Weakness Response—Finessing

Dealer East: N-S vulnerable

WEST	NORTH	EAST	SOUTH
		Pass	Pass
2♠	Pass	2NT	Pass
3♦	Pass	4♠	All pass

NORTH
♠ 10
♥ J 10 9 5 3 2
♦ 9 8
♣ A 8 7 2

WEST
♠ A K 7 5 2
♥ K Q
♦ A K J 6
♣ K Q

EAST
♠ 8 6 4 3
♥ 8 7
♦ 5 4 3 2
♠ 5 4 3

SOUTH
♠ Q J 9
♥ A 6 4
♦ Q 10 7
♣ J 10 9 6

Bidding: 2NT is the negative reply. East supports the spades later.

Lead: ♥J. Top of a sequence.

Play: When in, West plays A-K of spades. Normally leave the last trump out if it is a winner, but you need to reach dummy to take the diamond finesse. Concede a spade, win the return, cash one top diamond (in case the queen drops), cross to dummy with a trump, and lead a diamond, finessing the jack. The finesse for a queen is normally taken on the second round of the suit.

Hand 19: 2NT Opening—Suit response—Finessing

Dealer South: N-S vulnerable

NORTH
♠ A
♥ 8 6 5 3 2
♦ 7 4 3 2
♣ 7 5 3

WEST
♠ J 10 5 3
♥ 9 4
♦ J 10 8
♣ 10 9 8 6

EAST
♠ 9 7 4 2
♥ K 10 7
♦ 9 6 5
♣ A K Q

SOUTH
♠ K Q 8 6
♥ A Q J
♦ A K Q
♣ J 4 2

WEST	NORTH	EAST	SOUTH
			2NT
Pass	3♥	Pass	4♥
Pass	Pass	Pass	

Bidding: North's 3♥ shows *five* hearts and South has support. 3NT is beaten without difficulty as North's ace of spades entry is easily knocked out.

Lead: ♣A, normal from A-K suits.

Play: East cashes three clubs and switches to a spade. North wins and the best chance to avoid a heart loser is to finesse for the king. Low heart, low, queen . . . the finesse works. Ruff a spade to come back to hand and lead a low heart, low, finesse the jack. The ♥A then captures the king and declarer has the rest of the tricks.

Hand 20: Refusing to Over-ruff—Discarding a Loser Instead

Dealer West: Nil vulnerable

NORTH
♠ 8
♥ Q J 9 7 4
♦ Q 10 7 4 2
♣ 9 2

WEST
♠ 7 6
♥ 10 5 3 2
♦ 9 8 6 3
♣ Q 10 7

EAST
♠ A K Q 5 4 3 2
♥ A K
♦ A J
♣ J 8

SOUTH
♠ J 10 9
♥ 8 6
♦ K 5
♣ A K 6 5 4 3

WEST	NORTH	EAST	SOUTH
Pass	Pass	2♠	Pass
2NT	Pass	3♠	Pass
4♠	Pass	Pass	Pass

Bidding: East's 3♠ rebid shows at least six spades, so West raises to 4♠.

Lead: ♣A, normal from A-K suits.

Play: North's high-low, 9 then 2 in clubs, asks South to continue clubs. North ruffs the third club. If East over-ruffs, South's J-10-9 becomes a trump trick and, with a diamond to be lost, declarer is one down. This is unlucky for East but there is a perfectly good counter-measure. On the third club, declarer should not over-ruff. Discard the jack of diamonds and ten tricks are quite safe.

WEAK TWO BIDS AND THE 2♣ GAME FORCE

A popular method among tournament players is to use 2♣ as the only strong opening bid. The opening bids of 2♠, 2♥ and 2♦ are used as weak openings, like a pre-empt (Chapter 9), but with only a 6-card suit.

The 2♣ opening is artificial and forcing. Opener shows the long suit on the next round or rebids no-trumps with a balanced hand. The expectancy for the 2♣ opening is 23 HCP or more, or a hand with ten playing tricks or better. Players using this approach usually adjust the ranges for strong balanced hands as follows:

- **21–22 points balanced:** Open 2NT.
- **23–24 points balanced:** Open 2♣, rebid 2NT.
- **25–28 points balanced:** Open 2♣, rebid 3NT.

Responding to the 2♣ opening: With a poor hand (0–7 HCP), bid 2♦, the negative response. Any other reply is a positive response, showing 8 points or more, or a particularly strong 7 HCP, such as an ace plus a king or a suit headed by A-Q-J. A positive reply commits the partnership to game and usually leads to a slam.

After 2♣: 2♦, opener's 2NT rebid (23–24 points) is not forcing. Any other rebid by opener is forcing to game. Thus, the 2♣ opening is forcing to game except for the sequence 2♣: 2♦, 2NT. Bidding after the 2NT rebid follows the same structure as after a 2NT opening. If responder does bid over the 2NT rebid, the partnership is going to reach game.

Weak Two Bids: These show 6–10 HCP and a strong 6-card suit. With 11 HCP and a 6-card suit, you have enough for a one-opening. The suit should contain at least three points or at least two honors, in other words no worse than Q-J-x-x-x-x or Q-10-x-x-x-x. The weak two opening in first or second seat should not contain a void or two singletons or four cards in a side major suit.

With a singleton or a void in opener's suit, it is best to pass unless you have 16 HCP or more. A change of suit is forcing and implies you do not have support for opener's suit. Opener should raise a change of suit with doubleton support or better.

With support for opener's suit, look for game with about four winners and bid game with about five winners. With support and six winners or more, there are good prospects for a slam. Opener has about 5-6 tricks.

Part 2

AREAS OF BIDDING COMMON TO ALL STANDARD SYSTEMS

In general it is correct to say that when you state that you are playing a specific system this refers only to the meaning of your bids when your side opens the bidding and the responses to those opening bids. Almost invariably, the system you play will not stipulate the methods you should use when the opponents open the bidding. Also, it is usually only the meaning of opening bids at the one-level and two-level that are dictated by system requirements. Openings at higher levels are unaffected if a standard system is being played.

There are several areas of bidding which are common to all standard bidding systems. The areas which have a common treatment are:

- Slam bidding using the Blackwood Convention
- Pre-emptive openings of three or more in a suit
- Standard overcalls
- Takeout doubles

Each of these topics is examined in the following chapters.

Chapter 8
Slam Bidding

If you and your partner have the values for a slam, it is a losing approach not to bid the slam. Even if you fail occasionally, the rewards for slams are so great that you will be in front in the long run if you succeed in more than 50 percent of your slams. A small slam is worthwhile with 33 points or more and a grand slam should be bid if you have at least 37 points together.

However, there is more to bidding slams than just points. It is also vital that you cannot lose the first two tricks in a small slam and that there should be little risk of a loser in a grand slam. In particular, you should not lack two aces for a small slam, or an ace or a critical king or queen for a grand slam. As the 33 points for a small slam need not all be high card points, two aces might be missing. Likewise, even with 37 points, an ace or a key king or key queen could be missing. If you are in doubt, settle for a good small slam rather than take a risk for a grand slam.

If the partnership has 33+ HCP, two aces cannot be missing. If you have located a good trump fit or know that you should be in no-trumps, simply bid the slam you judge to be best without further ado. For example, if your partner opens 2NT and you hold 13 points with a 4-3-3-3 pattern, the commonsense bid is 6NT. You need no extra information to bid the slam. In other situations, you may know that there is enough strength for a slam and can tell that you cannot lose the first two tricks. For example:

♠ A Q J 8 6 4	Your partner passed, you opened 1♠ and your partner
♥ A 4	raised to 3♠. Since your partner passed initially, you can
♦ 5	expect the jump-raise to show support and 11–12 points.
♣ A K 3 2	Your hand, now worth 22, is enough for a small slam.

As you hold three aces and a singleton in the other suit, there is no threat of losing the first two tricks. Bid 6♠.

Most of the time you may know that there are enough points for a slam, but two aces could be missing. You will need to ask your partner for aces using the Blackwood Convention below. With Blackwood, you can check on how many aces your partner holds and also how many kings.

Before you use Blackwood, you should be confident of two things: firstly, that there are enough points for slam (aces do not cure a deficiency in points—even all four aces will produce only four tricks, while four aces and four kings add up to eight tricks), and secondly, you know your final destination: you know no-trumps is all right *or* you are aware of a strong trump fit, *or* you have a powerful self-sufficient trump suit.

BLACKWOOD 4NT—ASKING FOR ACES

A jump to 4NT, after a suit bid, asks your partner:
"How many aces do you have?"
The replies are:

5♣ = 0 or 4
5♦ = 1
5♥ = 2
5♠ = 3

After the answer to 4NT, 5NT asks your partner:
"How many kings do you hold?"
The replies are:

6♣ = 0
6♦ = 1
6♥ = 2
6♠ = 3
6NT = 4

To use the 5NT ask for kings, you should have ambitions for a grand slam. The partnership should have the values for a grand slam, a strong trump suit, and there should not be any aces missing. In other words, the use of 5NT asking for kings promises that the partnership holds all the aces.

4NT is usually Blackwood asking for aces, but if 4NT is used as an immediate response to an opening bid of no-trumps (e.g., 1NT: 4NT or 2NT: 4NT, or a response or a rebid in no-trumps) this is not used as Blackwood, but as an invitation to 6NT. Opener is asked to pass with a minimum opening and to bid on with more than minimum points. If you wish to check on aces after an opening bid of no-trumps, you will need to bid a suit first (e.g., 1NT: 3♥ or 2NT: 3♦) and then bid 4NT later. It is normally asking for aces if the preceding bid was a suit bid.

EXERCISES ON SLAM BIDDING

A. In each of the following auctions you are South with the hand shown.
Would you say that you are in the slam zone or the game zone?

1.	♠ K 10 9 6 4	2.	♠ K 6 3	3.	♠ K Q 7
	♥ K Q 5		♥ K 9		♥ K J 4 3
	♦ A 9 7 3		♦ Q 10 7 6 5 3		♦ A 8 7
	♣ 4		♣ A 2		♣ J 4 3

N	S	N	S	N	S
2NT	?	2♥	?	1NT	?

4.	♠ A K J	5.	♠ Q 5	6.	♠ 6
	♥ K Q 10 9 7 6		♥ A Q 8 4 3		♥ K 9
	♦ K Q		♦ K J 6 2		♦ A 4 3 2
	♣ J 6		♣ A J		♣ A K Q 7 6 2

N	S	N	S	N	S
	1♥		1♥	1♥	2♣
4♥	?	3♥	?	3♥	?

B. What should South call next in each of these auctions?

1.	♠ A J 8 3	2.	♠ A 8 7	3.	♠ K Q 7
	♥ A 6		♥ A 4		♥ K Q 8 4 3
	♦ A Q J 4 2		♦ A J 9 4		♦ 7
	♣ 8 3		♣ A 7 4 3		♣ A K Q 3

N	S	N	S	N	S
	1♦		1NT		1♥
1♠	3♠	3♥	4♥	3♥	4NT
4NT	?	4NT	?	5♦	?

4.	♠ J 4 3 2	5.	♠ K 8 4	6.	♠ K J 3
	♥ K 8 5		♥ A 9		♥ 6 4 2
	♦ 3		♦ Q 9 8 6 2		♦ A K 5 2
	♣ A K J 6 4		♣ K 8 6		♣ A 8 3

N	S	N	S	N	S
1♥	2♣	1♥	2♦	1♥	3NT
2♦	3♥	3♥	4♥	4♣	4♥
4NT	?	4NT	5♦	4NT	5♥
		5♥	?	5NT	?

C. You hold: What is your next call in each of these auctions?

♠ K Q J 5 3
♥ A Q J 4 2
♦ K Q
♣ 6

a. You	Ptnr.	b. You	Ptnr.	c. You	Ptnr.
1♠	3♠	1♠	3♠		1♣
4NT	5♥	4NT	5♠	1♠	3♠
?		5NT	6♦	4NT	5♠
		?		5NT	6♥
				?	

D. You hold: What is your next call in each of these auctions?

♠ A 9 5
♥ A J 6 3 2
♦ - - -
♣ Q J 8 7 6

a. You	Ptnr.	b. You	Ptnr.	c. You	Ptnr.
1♥	4NT		1♠	1♥	1♠
5♥	6♦	2♥	4NT	2♣	4NT
?		5♥	6♦	5♥	5♠
		?		?	

E. You hold: What is your next call in each of these auctions?

♠ A 8 4 3 2
♥ K Q 10
♦ 6
♣ K Q J 3

a. You	Ptnr.	b. You	Ptnr.	c. You	Ptnr.
1♠	2♣	1♠	2♦	1♠	2♥
4♣	4NT	3♣	5♠	4♥	5♥
5♦	5♥				
?					

PARTNERSHIP BIDDING PRACTICE

West is the dealer on each hand. How should the bidding go?

	WEST		EAST		WEST		EAST
57.	♠ A K J 7 4 ♥ A K Q 3 ♦ A J ♣ J 3	57.	♠ 10 3 ♥ J 8 ♦ K Q 6 2 ♣ K Q 9 7 4	60.	♠ A Q J 7 6 ♥ A Q J 5 ♦ K 3 ♣ K 9	60.	♠ 9 5 ♥ K 7 4 3 ♦ A Q 7 ♣ A 8 5 4
58.	♠ Q J 8 ♥ K Q 9 7 ♦ A K Q ♣ 8 7 2	58.	♠ A 6 4 ♥ A J 2 ♦ 8 7 4 2 ♣ A K Q	61.	♠ K 9 8 ♥ Q J 7 ♦ A Q 6 ♣ A K Q 6	61.	♠ A Q 6 ♥ A K 3 ♦ K J 5 2 ♣ 9 5 4
59.	♠ K 6 ♥ 9 5 3 2 ♦ K 7 4 ♣ A 8 4 2	59.	♠ A Q J ♥ A K Q 8 7 6 ♦ A Q 3 ♣ K	62.	♠ A J ♥ A K Q J 8 4 ♦ A K Q 2 ♣ A	62.	♠ K 9 4 ♥ 5 3 2 ♦ 8 7 5 ♣ K 8 6 2

PLAY HANDS ON SLAM BIDDING

Hand 21: 2NT Opening—Setting Up Extra Tricks—Finessing

Dealer North: Nil vulnerable

NORTH
- ♠ 9 6 5 2
- ♥ J 10 9 4 3
- ♦ 6 5 2
- ♣ 10

WEST
- ♠ Q J 4
- ♥ K Q 6
- ♦ K 7 4
- ♣ J 8 3 2

EAST
- ♠ A K 7
- ♥ A 8 2
- ♦ A Q 3
- ♣ K Q 5 4

SOUTH
- ♠ 10 8 3
- ♥ 7 5
- ♦ J 10 9 8
- ♣ A 9 7 6

WEST	NORTH	EAST	SOUTH
	Pass	2NT	Pass
6NT	Pass	Pass	Pass

Bidding: With 12 HCP opposite 2NT 21-22, West has just enough for slam.

Lead: ♦J. Top of a sequence.

Play: With 9 tricks outside clubs, 3 club tricks are needed to succeed. Win the lead in dummy and play a club to the King. If it wins continue with the ♣Q, while if the ♣K is taken by the ace, win the return and cash the ♣Q. When North shows out on the second club, take a finesse of dummy's ♣8 on the next round.

Wrong play: Playing winners in the other suits before tackling clubs.

Hand 22: Leaving the Top Trump out While You Discard a Loser

Dealer East: N-S vulnerable

NORTH
- ♠ J 6
- ♥ 9 7 5 3 2
- ♦ A 2
- ♣ A Q J 5

WEST
- ♠ 9 8 7 5 4 3
- ♥ 10
- ♦ 10 9 3
- ♣ 10 4 3

EAST
- ♠ K Q 10
- ♥ Q J 8
- ♦ 8 4
- ♣ K 9 7 6 2

SOUTH
- ♠ A 2
- ♥ A K 6 4
- ♦ K Q J 7 6 5
- ♣ 8

WEST	NORTH	EAST	SOUTH
		Pass	1♦
Pass	1♥	Pass	4♥
Pass	4NT	Pass	5♥
Pass	6♥	All pass	

Bidding: 4♥ showed enough for game opposite 6 points, so that South must have 19–20 points or more. With 14 points, North bids to a slam after checking on aces.

Lead: ♠K. The lead from K-Q-10 or K-Q-x is the king.

Play: Win the ♠A. Play the A-K of hearts, the ♦A, a diamond to the king and on the third diamond, discard your spade loser. East ruffs, but the spade loser has been eliminated.

Hand 23: Rejecting a Finesse—Delaying Trumps—Discarding a Loser

Dealer South: Both vulnerable

WEST	NORTH	EAST	SOUTH
			Pass
Pass	2♠	Pass	3♥
Pass	4NT	Pass	5♦
Pass	6♥	All pass	

```
                NORTH
                ♠ A K Q J 2
                ♥ K Q J 4
                ♦ A Q J
                ♣ 2
WEST                        EAST
♠ 10 8                      ♠ 9 6 5 4 3
♥ 6                         ♥ A 8
♦ 10 9 8 7 5 4              ♦ K 2
♣ Q 10 8 7                  ♣ 9 6 5 4
                SOUTH
                ♠ 7
                ♥ 10 9 7 5 3 2
                ♦ 6 3
                ♣ A K J 3
```

Bidding: South's 3♥, a positive reply with 5+ hearts, is enough for North to check on aces and bid slam.

Lead: ♦10. Top of a sequence.

Play: Win the ♦A, play ♠A-K to discard the diamond loser and then lead trumps. Later the last trump is drawn and losing clubs are ruffed or discarded on the spade winners.

Wrong play: (1) Taking the unnecessary diamond finesse at trick 1. (2) Playing trumps before taking a discard. East wins ♥A, cashes ♦K.

Hand 24: Card Combinations—Setting up Winners to Discard Losers

Dealer West: Nil vulnerable

WEST	NORTH	EAST	SOUTH
1♠	Pass	3♠	Pass
4NT	Pass	5♦	Pass
6♠	Pass	Pass	Pass

```
                NORTH
                ♠ Q 10 9
                ♥ J 10 9 8
                ♦ Q 10 9
                ♣ 9 6 5
WEST                        EAST
♠ K 8 6 5 4 2               ♠ A J 7 3
♥ A                         ♥ K Q
♦ A K 5 4                   ♦ 8 7 3
♣ K Q                       ♣ J 10 8 4
                SOUTH
                ♠ - - -
                ♥ 7 6 5 4 3 2
                ♦ J 6 2
                ♣ A 7 3 2
```

Bidding: After East's 3♠ showed 10–12 points and support, West re-values to 23 points, checks on aces, and bids the small slam.

Lead: ♥J. Top of a sequence.

Play: Win the ♥A, play ♠K next, preserving the A-J tenace in dummy just in case a finesse is needed. When South shows out, finesse the ♠J, cash the ♠A to draw the last trump and then lead a club to knock out the ace. Later you can discard two diamond losers on the winners in dummy.

Chapter 9
Pre-emptive Opening Bids

Without interference, most pairs with a little experience can bid well enough to the best spot most of the time. Information is exchanged by the partnership's dialogue. For example, 1♥: 2♣, 2♦: 2♥, 4♥ can be translated into: "I have hearts": "What about clubs?" "No, I have diamonds, too": "Oh, I prefer your hearts." "All right, let's try 4♥ then."

Imagine that before the above dialogue took place you had opened 3♠. What happens to their dialogue? Opening bids of 3-in-a-suit or 4-in-a-suit or 5♣ or 5♦ are called pre-empts, because by getting in first you aim to shut out the opponents.

Pre-empts force the opposition into guessing what to do. Their decisions have to be made without any clear knowledge of what is held by their partner. When they have to guess at the contract, they will sometimes make the wrong guess. That is your profit.

A pre-emptive bid is made on the first round of bidding. There is no such concept as a pre-emptive rebid, since if the opponents have not entered the bidding on the first round, there is no need to shut them out. A pre-empt can be made in any position, by opener, by responder, or by either defender. Pre-empts are more effective the sooner they are made, as that reduces the amount of information the opponents can exchange. Therefore, pre-empt as high as you dare as early as possible. Once you have pre-empted, do not bid again unless your partner makes a forcing bid.

A pre-emptive bid skips two or more levels of bidding. For example, opening 3♦ is a pre-empt because it skips over 1♦ and 2♦. Likewise, 1♣: 3♦ is a pre-empt because it skips over 1♦ and 2♦, but, 1♠: 3♦ would not be a pre-empt, as it skips over only one level, the 2♦ bid. The 3♦ response here is a jump-shift, the most powerful response possible.

The normal pre-empt is usually 6-10 HCP and has a strong 7+ suit.

A pre-emptive opening may have fewer than 6 points if it contains the right number of playing tricks (see below), but in practice, this is very rare. It may also be a very powerful 6-card suit, but this is rare, too. Do not pre-empt if you have a 4-card or longer major as a second suit.

When you have a hand suitable for a pre-empt, you may open with a bid of 3 or a bid of 4 (and if your suit is a minor, you may even begin with a bid of 5♣ or 5♦). How can you judge whether you should open with a 3-bid or with a higher bid? The answer depends on the number of playing tricks you hold. The Rule of 3 and 2 states: "Count your playing tricks and add 3 tricks if not vulnerable, 2 tricks if vulnerable. Make the opening bid corresponding to this total number of tricks." In other words:

- With 6 playing tricks, open 3 if not vulnerable, pass if vulnerable.
- With 7 playing tricks, open 4 if not vulnerable, open 3 if vulnerable.
- With 8 playing tricks: Not vulnerable, open 4 if your suit is a major and 5 if your suit is a minor. If vulnerable, open 4 in either case.
- With 9 playing tricks, open 4 if your suit is a major, 5 if a minor.

How to Count Your Playing Tricks

(1) Count every card after the third card in a suit as one playing trick.

(2) In the top three cards of each suit, each ace and each king = one trick.

(3) Count each queen as a trick if there is a second honor card in that suit.

(4) Count no trick for a singleton king, singleton queen, or queen doubleton. Count only one trick for holding K-Q doubleton.

RESPONDING TO YOUR PARTNER'S PRE-EMPTIVE OPENING

(1) Assess how many tricks your partner has shown by deducting three if your side is not vulnerable or two if your side is vulnerable.

(2) Add to this your own "quick tricks": Count the A, K, or Q of your partner's suit as one trick each. In other suits, count A-K as 2, A-Q as 1½, A as 1, K-Q as 1, and K as ½. If you have support for opener's suit, count an outside singleton as one trick and an outside void as two.

(3) If the total is less than your partner needs or just enough for the contract, pass.

(4) If the total is more than your partner needs, you should bid on to game (but if your partner's bid is already a game, you would pass). If the total is 12 or more, bid to a slam, but check via 4NT that two aces are not missing.

(5) Over an opening bid of 3♣ or 3♦, you may try 3NT with a strong balanced hand and at least one stopper in each of the outside suits.

(6) Over other opening pre-empts, prefer to stick with your partner's suit unless you have a strong hand and a long, powerful suit of your own. A change of suit below game in response to a pre-empt is forcing.

(7) Do not rescue your partner from a pre-empt. With a weak hand, pass.

EXERCISES ON PRE-EMPTIVE BIDDING

A. Pre-empts are based on playing trick potential. How many tricks would you expect to win with each of these suits as trumps?

1.	A K Q x x x x x	**7.**	A Q x x x x x	**13.**	K J x x x x x x
2.	A K Q x x x x	**8.**	A K x x x x x	**14.**	K x x x x x x
3.	A K Q x x x	**9.**	A J x x x x	**15.**	Q J 10 x x x x
4.	A K J x x x x x	**10.**	A x x x x x x	**16.**	Q x x x x x x x
5.	A K J x x x x	**11.**	K Q J x x x x	**17.**	J x x x x x x
6.	A Q J x x x x	**12.**	K Q x x x x x x	**18.**	x x x x x x x x x

B. You are dealer. What action do you take with these hands if you are: (i) not vulnerable? (ii) vulnerable?

1. ♠ Q J 10 8 7 4 2
   ♥ 5
   ♦ K Q J
   ♣ 5 4

2. ♠ 8
   ♥ K Q J 9 7 6 5 4
   ♦ 4 3
   ♣ 3 2

3. ♠ K 3
   ♥ 5 4
   ♦ 8 7
   ♣ A K J 9 8 6 2

4. ♠ 3 2
   ♥ - - -
   ♦ A K Q 9 8 7 5 4 2
   ♣ 5 2

5. ♠ K J 10 7 6 5 4
   ♥ 6
   ♦ Q J 10 9 6
   ♣ - - -

6. ♠ 5
   ♥ 4 3
   ♦ 7 4 3 2
   ♣ A K Q 7 6 4

7. ♠ K Q J 8 7
   ♥ 5
   ♦ Q J 10 6
   ♣ 4 3 2

8. ♠ K 6 3 2
   ♥ 9
   ♦ 3
   ♣ A 8 7 6 4 3 2

9. ♠ J 9 8 6 5 4
   ♥ A K 3
   ♦ 9 8 7
   ♣ 3

10. ♠ A K 8 7 6 4
    ♥ Q 9 7 6 3
    ♦ 2
    ♣ 6

11. ♠ A 5
    ♥ A K Q 9 7 6 3
    ♦ Q 9 7
    ♣ 2

12. ♠ 6 5
    ♥ A K Q 9 7 6 3
    ♦ 9 7 3
    ♣ 2

13. ♠ 4
    ♥ J 9 7 6 4 3 2
    ♦ A 2
    ♣ J 8 6

14. ♠ A K Q J 5 3 2
    ♥ A K
    ♦ Q 9 7
    ♣ A

15. ♠ K Q J 6 5 3 2
    ♥ 4
    ♦ 2
    ♣ Q 10 7 3

C. Your partner opens 3♥. Your response: (i) not vulnerable? (ii) vulnerable?

1. ♠ A J 9 8 7	2. ♠ A J 9 8 6 4	3. ♠ A K 5 4 3
♥ 5 3	♥ 3	♥ - - -
♦ Q J 7 6	♦ Q J 7	♦ J 8 7 4 3
♣ 8 5	♣ 6 5 2	♣ 9 7 6
4. ♠ A K J 8 7 2	5. ♠ A 8 7	6. ♠ 7
♥ 5	♥ Q 7 6	♥ Q 4 3
♦ A Q J	♦ K 8 3	♦ A K 8 4 3
♣ J 3 2	♣ 6 5 4 2	♣ J 6 3 2
7. ♠ A Q J	8. ♠ A K 6 5 3 2	9. ♠ A K J 4 3
♥ 5 4 3	♥ 4 3	♥ 9 7
♦ Q J 10 6	♦ A 7	♦ K Q J 7 6
♣ K Q 10	♣ Q J 7	♣ 2
10. ♠ K 8 7 6 4	11. ♠ A 5	12. ♠ A 6 5
♥ 3	♥ K 7 6 4	♥ K 9 4
♦ A J 7 6 5 2	♦ A 9 7	♦ A K Q 8 7 2
♣ 4	♣ A K Q J	♣ 5

Partnership Bidding Practice

West is the dealer, neither side vulnerable. How should the bidding go?

WEST	EAST	WEST	EAST
63.	**63.**	**66.**	**66.**
♠ K Q J 8 6 4 3	♠ 10 2	♠ A 7 6	♠ 4
♥ 8 4	♥ A K 6	♥ 7	♥ K Q J 8 6 5 2
♦ 4 3	♦ A K 7 5	♦ A J 8 4 3	♦ 9 6
♣ 9 7	♣ 8 6 5 4	♣ 6 5 4 2	♣ 8 7 3
64.	**64.**	**67.**	**67.**
♠ 8	♠ A Q 3	♠ A Q J 9 6 4 3 2	♠ K 8 7
♥ 10 6	♥ A J 7 2	♥ 9 4	♥ 7
♦ A Q J 7 6 5 4	♦ 8 3 2	♦ 8	♦ A K 4 3
♣ 7 6 2	♣ A J 10	♣ 9 7	♣ A 8 6 4 3
65.	**65.**	**68.**	**68.**
♠ 9 3	♠ A K 7 6 5 4	♠ 8 2	♠ A K Q
♥ 8	♥ A 9 5	♥ A 4	♥ K Q J 7 5 3 2
♦ A K J 7 5 3 2	♦ 8	♦ K Q 9 7 4 3 2	♦ 6
♣ 9 5 3	♣ A Q 4	♣ 7 5	♣ A Q

PLAY HANDS ON PRE-EMPTIVE BIDDING

Hand 25: Shut-out Opening—Establishing a Second Suit in Hand

Dealer North: Nil vulnerable

WEST	NORTH	EAST	SOUTH
			4♠
		All pass	

NORTH
♠ A K Q 9 7 6 5
♥ 2
♦ 8
♣ 9 8 7 3

WEST
♠ J 8 3
♥ 10 9 6 5 4
♦ K Q 10
♣ A K

EAST
♠ 10
♥ K Q J 8 3
♦ A J 5
♣ 6 5 4 2

SOUTH
♠ 4 2
♥ A 7
♦ 9 7 6 4 3 2
♣ Q J 10

Bidding: With 7 tricks not vulnerable, North has enough to open 4♠ rather than 3♠. Neither East nor West is strong enough to bid over that. Note that if West were the dealer, West would open 1♥ and over North's 4♠ overcall, East would compete to 5♥, which would succeed. North's 4♠ opening has shut East-West out of the game they could make.

Lead: ♥K. Top of a sequence.

Play: Win ♥A, draw trumps in three rounds and then lead clubs at each opportunity to set up two extra tricks after the ♣A-K are forced out.

Hand 26: Play from Dummy At Trick 1—Establishing a Long Suit

Dealer East: N-S vulnerable

WEST	NORTH	EAST	SOUTH
		3♣	Pass
3NT	Pass	Pass	Pass

NORTH
♠ K Q 7 6
♥ K 10 8 7 3
♦ J 9 8
♣ 2

WEST
♠ A 10 9 3
♥ A 6 5
♦ A K 10
♣ 9 5 4

EAST
♠ 4 2
♥ Q 4
♦ 6 3
♣ K Q J 8 7 6 3

SOUTH
♠ J 8 5
♥ J 9 2
♦ Q 7 5 4 2
♣ A 10

Bidding: With six playing tricks and not vulnerable, East may open 3♣. With a balanced hand, all outside suits covered and four tricks opposite East's six, West should choose 3NT.

Lead: ♥7. Fourth-highest.

Play: Play the ♥Q from dummy, hoping to win the trick (when North has the king). When the ♥Q holds, lead clubs to force out the ace. Once the ♣A has gone, dummy's clubs are high. South should return a heart, partner's suit, but West wins and cashes the clubs and other winners.

Hand 27: Slam Bidding after a Pre-empt—Setting up a Long Suit

Dealer South: Both vulnerable

WEST	NORTH	EAST	SOUTH
			4♦
Pass	4NT	Pass	5♦
Pass	6♦	All pass	

NORTH
♠ J
♥ A Q J
♦ K 10 9
♣ A 9 8 7 6 3

WEST
♠ K 10 9 5 4 3
♥ 9 8 6
♦ - - -
♣ K Q J 4

EAST
♠ A Q 7 6 2
♥ K 5 4 3 2
♦ 7
♣ 10 2

SOUTH
♠ 8
♥ 10 7
♦ A Q J 8 6 5 4 3 2
♣ 5

Bidding: With eight tricks vulnerable, South opens 4♦ rather than 3♦. With three sure winners and potential for another in three other suits, North bids to slam after checking on aces.

Lead: ♣K. Top of a sequence.

Play: The best play is to set up the club suit. Win ♣A, ruff a club high, diamond to dummy's 9, ruff a club, diamond to dummy's 10, ruff a club. The last two clubs in dummy are high. Diamond to the king (or a heart to the ace) and play the clubs on which a spade and a heart are discarded.

Hand 28: Pre-emptive Opening—Counting Tricks—Slam Bidding

Dealer West: Nil vulnerable

WEST	NORTH	EAST	SOUTH
3♥	Pass	4NT	Pass
5♦	Pass	7NT	All pass

NORTH
♠ 10 6 4 3 2
♥ - - -
♦ K 9 3 2
♣ 10 8 7 6

WEST
♠ 7
♥ A 9 8 7 6 3 2
♦ Q J 10
♣ 4 3

EAST
♠ A 9 5
♥ K 10 5 4
♦ A 6
♣ A K Q J

SOUTH
♠ K Q J 8
♥ Q J
♦ 8 7 5 4
♣ 9 5 2

Bidding: With five playing tricks in hearts and one in diamonds, West opens 3♥ not vulnerable. East has enough for a slam and after finding the missing ace, East counts tricks: one in spades, seven in hearts (given that West has seven hearts to the ace), one in diamonds and four in clubs. With 13 top winners, choose 7NT, mainly because you eliminate the risk of the opening lead being ruffed.

Lead: ♠K. Top of a sequence.

Play: Win and play out the hearts, being careful to play the ♥10 early, so that the hearts are not blocked.

Chapter 10

Standard Overcalls

With normal luck, your side will open the bidding only half the time. This chapter and the next are concerned with the actions you may take after the bidding has been opened by the other side. There is only one opening bid in each auction, the first bid made, and there is only one opening bidder. The partner of the opening bidder is the responder and the opposing side is known as "the defenders." Their bidding is called "defensive bidding." A bid made by a defender is an "overcall" (or an "interpose"), but not an opening. There is no such concept as "opening for your side" after the other side has made a bid. The principles for defensive bidding are not the same as for opening the bidding and it is essential to appreciate the differences.

THE 1NT OVERCALL

This shows a balanced hand, 15-18 points, and at least one stopper in their suit. The minimum holdings which qualify as a stopper are the ace, K-x, Q-x-x or J-x-x-x, i.e., a holding where if they lead their suit from the top, you will win a trick in that suit. Bidding after the 1NT overcall follows the same structure as after an opening bid of 1NT (see Chapter 3).

THE SUIT OVERCALL

The great difference between opening the bidding (constructive bidding) and bidding after the opponents have opened (competitive bidding) is this: With 13 points or more, you would always *open* the bidding, yet if they have already opened the bidding you should pass *unless your hand fits the requirements for an overcall or for a takeout double* (see Chapter 11). Thus, if they have opened, there is no obligation for you to bid, even if you have 13 points or 15 points or 17 points . . . The most common strong hands on which you would pass are balanced hands up to 14 points (too weak for a 1NT overcall) if they are not suitable for a takeout double, and those hands which have length and strength in a suit bid by the opponents.

While there are no suit quality requirements for *opening* and while you might *open* in a very weak suit, *overcalls in a suit* are based on strong suits, at least five cards long. The essence of the overcall is the long, strong suit. If your suit is strong, you may make an overcall even with as few as 8 or 9 HCP. Points are less important than suit quality.

A suit overcall at the 1-level shows:
- **A strong suit, at least five cards long, and**
- **8–16 HCP.**

A suit overcall at the 2-level (not a jump-overcall) shows:
- **A strong suit, at least five cards long, and**
- **10–16 HCP.**

Thus, an overcall might be as strong as a minimum opening hand, but it need not be that strong. It can be quite weak in high cards. Just how good must a suit be to qualify as a "strong suit?" An excellent guide for overcalls and for pre-emptive openings is the **Suit Quality Test**:

Count the number of cards in the suit you wish to bid. Add the number of honor cards in that suit (but count the jack or ten as a full honor only if the suit also contains at least one higher honor).

The total is the number of tricks for which you may bid that suit. Thus, if the total is 7, you may bid your suit at the 1-level. If the total is 8, you may bid your suit at the 1-level, or the 2-level if necessary. If the total is 9, you may bid your suit at the 1-level, the 2-level or, if necessary, the 3-level.

RESPONDING TO A SUIT OVERCALL

Responding to a suit overcall is like responding to an opening bid. The point ranges are usually the same, but you are not obliged to reply with 6–7 points if you do not have support for your partner. You need only three trumps to support your partner's overcall, whether it is in a major suit or a minor. Raising partner shows 6–10 points, a jump-raise = 11–14 HCP and a major-suit raise from the one to four would be based on 15+ HCP. With their suit stopped, you may reply 1NT (8–11 points), 2NT (12–15) or 3NT (16–18). A change of suit at the 1-level = 8+ points, while at the 2-level it would show 10+ points, just like a normal 2-level response.

Supporting your partner or bidding no-trumps is not forcing, but it is sensible to play change of suit as forcing for one round. A jump-shift in reply to an overcall = 16+ points, a good 5+ suit and is forcing to game.

After your partner has replied to your overcall you may pass with a minimum overcall if you have nothing worthwhile to add, but keep bidding if:

(a) Your partner's reply was forcing, *or*

(b) You have a maximum overcall (in the 13–16 point zone), *or*

(c) You are minimum but you have something extra worth showing.

THE JUMP-OVERCALL

A jump-overcall is an overcall of one more than the minimum required, for example, (1♣): 2♥ or (1♦): 3♣. The jump-overcall shows a good six-card or longer suit and 15 points or more, usually 15–18 points. This method is known as strong jump-overcalls. (Other methods which are in use are weak jump-overcalls–6–10 HCP and a six-card or longer suit–and intermediate jump-overcalls–11–14 HCP and a six-card or longer suit.) Assume that you are using strong jump-overcalls unless you and your partner have specifically agreed to use one of the other methods.

One-suited hands are normally shown simply by bidding your long suit. However, hands with a good five-card suit but which are too strong for a simple overcall are shown by a double first, followed by a bid of your long suit on the next round (see Chapter 11).

RESPONDING TO A STRONG JUMP-OVERCALL

You should respond to a strong jump-overcall with 6 points or more.

If your partner's suit is a major, the first priority is to raise that major. Only two trumps are needed to raise a jump-overcall since the suit will be at least six cards long. With 10 points or more, you should raise a major suit jump-overcall from the 2-level to the 4-level. Without support, bid the other major with at least five cards there, or bid no-trumps if you have their suit stopped. Your last choice would be to introduce a minor suit, but if there is nothing else available, bid a minor.

If your partner's suit is a minor, bid a long major as first priority, no-trumps as your second choice and raise the minor or bid the other minor as your last choice. A change of suit in reply to a jump-overcall is forcing. With a strong hand and no clear-cut action, you may force your partner to keep bidding if you bid the enemy suit. This is an artificial, forcing bid.

DOUBLE AND TRIPLE JUMP-OVERCALLS

A double or triple jump-overcall, such as (1♣): 3♠ or (1♦): 4♥, is a pre-empt, as it skips over two or more levels of bidding. Pre-emptive jump-overcalls follow the same rules as a pre-emptive opening. The suit should be strong with at least seven cards, conforming to the **Suit Quality Test**. The Rule of 3 and 2 applies and the normal high card strength is 6–10 points. However, pre-emptive overcalls of 4♥ or 4♠ are more flexible and the strength can be up to 15 HCP (since your bid is already game and slam is so unlikely after they have opened the bidding).

EXERCISES ON OVERCALLS

A. Your right-hand opponent opens 1♥. Do you bid or pass on the following hands? If you decide to bid, what bid do you make?

1.	2.	3.	4.
♠ A 7	♠ A 9	♠ A 7 5 2	♠ K Q
♥ Q 5 2	♥ K Q 8 3	♥ Q 8	♥ A K J 9 7
♦ K J 4 2	♦ A J 7	♦ Q 7 6 5 3	♦ 9 4 3 2
♣ K J 6 4	♣ Q J 8 2	♣ K 3	♣ J 2

B. Your right-hand opponent opens 1♣. What action do you take?

1.	2.	3.
♠ K Q 9 7 4 3	♠ K Q J 7 6	♠ K Q 9 7
♥ 7 6 4	♥ 7	♥ 3
♦ K 8 2	♦ A 5 4 2	♦ A 8 7 2
♣ 6	♣ 7 6 5	♣ Q 7 6 3

4.	5.	6.
♠ 7	♠ A	♠ A Q J 10 7 5 4
♥ A J 7 2	♥ A J 7 2	♥ 6
♦ A Q J 9 3	♦ J 8 5 3 2	♦ Q 9 5 3
♣ 7 6 3	♣ Q 9 7	♣ 7

7.	8.	9.
♠ A Q 9 4 2	♠ A Q	♠ A Q
♥ 7	♥ A K J 7 5 4	♥ 9 7 5 3 2
♦ A K J 5 3	♦ Q 4 3	♦ K Q
♣ 6 2	♣ 6 2	♣ Q 8 7 2

C. Your right-hand opponent opens 1♠. What action do you take?

1.	2.	3.
♠ K 7	♠ K 7	♠ 7 6
♥ 6 4	♥ A Q	♥ K 4
♦ A Q J 7 3 2	♦ Q 8 6 3 2	♦ A 5 4
♣ 7 6 3	♣ Q 9 8 6	♣ A K Q J 7 5

4. ♠ A Q
   ♥ 8 5 3
   ♦ A 5
   ♣ A K Q J 4 3

5. ♠ 7
   ♥ A 10 9 8 6 2
   ♦ A K J 2
   ♣ 8 3

6. ♠ A K 10 7 4
   ♥ K
   ♦ Q 9 7
   ♣ J 8 6 3

7. ♠ - - -
   ♥ 7 6
   ♦ K Q J 9 8 6 4 3
   ♣ A J 10

8. ♠ - - -
   ♥ 7 6 4
   ♦ K Q J 9 6 5
   ♣ K 9 6 2

9. ♠ J 8 6 4
   ♥ 6 2
   ♦ Q 7
   ♣ A K 8 4 2

D. N   E   S   W
    1♦ No 1♥ ?

The bidding has started as on the left.
What action should West take on these hands?

1. ♠ A J 7 4
   ♥ J 5 2
   ♦ K Q 5 2
   ♣ A 7

2. ♠ K Q J 8 4
   ♥ A Q
   ♦ 5 4 3 2
   ♣ 7 6

3. ♠ Q J 10 9 7 4 3
   ♥ 6
   ♦ - - -
   ♣ A 8 4 3 2

E. N   E   S   W
    1♠ No 2♣ ?

The bidding has started as on the left.
What should West take on these hands?

1. ♠ K 6 3 2
   ♥ Q J 8 2
   ♦ A K 7
   ♣ K Q

2. ♠ 6
   ♥ K Q J 10 9 4 3
   ♦ K Q 3
   ♣ A Q

3. ♠ A Q 9 7
   ♥ A 4 3
   ♦ 9 2
   ♣ K Q J 5

F. N   E   S   W
    1♣ 1♥ No ?

The bidding has started as on the left.
What should West take on these hands?

1. ♠ K 8 4 3
   ♥ 7 6
   ♦ K 7 6 3
   ♣ 9 4 3

2. ♠ 6
   ♥ K 8 4 3 2
   ♦ A K 8 6 5
   ♣ 7 4

3. ♠ 6 4
   ♥ K 8 4 3
   ♦ A 8 5 4 2
   ♣ 7 2

4. ♠ Q 6
   ♥ K 8 4
   ♦ A K 8 5 3
   ♣ 7 5 2

5. ♠ A 6 5
   ♥ 3
   ♦ K Q J 6 4 2
   ♣ 7 6 3

6. ♠ A 9 7
   ♥ 7 6
   ♦ K 10 8 6
   ♣ Q J 9 4

7. ♠ A J 8
    ♥ Q 4 3
    ♦ J 10 7 4
    ♣ K Q 10

8. ♠ A Q 9 7 4 3
    ♥ 7 2
    ♦ K 8 4
    ♣ 6 3

9. ♠ A Q 8
    ♥ K 7
    ♦ Q J 10 7
    ♣ K Q 8 6

G. | N | E | S | W |
    |---|---|---|---|
    | 1♥ | 2♠ | No | ? |

East's 2♠ is a strong jump-overcall.
What should West do with these hands?

1. ♠ 10 7 6
    ♥ Q 9
    ♦ A 8 7 4 2
    ♣ 5 4 3

2. ♠ K 7 4 2
    ♥ 4
    ♦ Q J 9 5
    ♣ 8 7 5 2

3. ♠ 7 6
    ♥ K Q 10
    ♦ 8 7 6 4 2
    ♣ Q 10 3

Partnership Bidding Practice Featuring Overcalls

There is no North-South bidding other than that shown.

WEST	EAST	WEST	EAST
69.	**69.**	**74.**	**74.**
S. opens 1♣.	S. opens 1♣.	N. opens 1♥.	N. opens 1♥.
♠ A J 8	♠ K Q 3	♠ A J	♠ K Q 9 7 6 2
♥ K Q 9 8 6 3	♥ 7 5	♥ 7 5 4 2	♥ 9 3
♦ 7 6 2	♦ J 9 8 3	♦ K Q 3	♦ A 8
♣ 8	♣ A 9 7 4	♣ 8 6 4 2	♣ A K 5

WEST	EAST	WEST	EAST
70.	**70.**	**75.**	**75.**
S. opens 1♣.	S. opens 1♣.	N. opens 1♥.	N. opens 1♥.
♠ A Q 7	♠ K J	♠ Q J 7 6 4	♠ A 9 3
♥ K Q	♥ J 1 0 9 7 4 2	♥ 7	♥ 6 2
♦ A 9 8 3	♦ K Q 6 2	♦ Q 9 3	♦ A K J 8 7 4
♣ Q 8 7 2	♣ 3	♣ A J 8 6	♣ 9 3

WEST	EAST	WEST	EAST
71.	**71.**	**76.**	**76.**
N. opens 1♦.	N. opens 1♦.	S. opens 1♠.	S. opens 1♠.
♠ A 7 6	♠ K 8 3	♠ 7 5	♠ K 8 4 2
♥ K Q 3	♥ A J 9 7 6 4	♥ A 8 3	♥ K 9 7
♦ J 8 7 4	♦ A Q	♦ 7 6	♦ A J 5 2
♣ 7 3 2	♣ Q 4	♣ A K J 9 3 2	♣ Q 8

WEST	EAST	WEST	EAST
72.	**72.**	**77.**	**77.**
N. opens 1♦.	N. opens 1♦.	S. opens 1♠.	S. opens 1♠.
♠ K Q J	♠ A 7 4	♠ 6 4 3 2	♠ 9
♥ 9 8 5 2	♥ K Q J 7 3	♥ A 8	♥ K Q J 7 5 4
♦ Q 3	♦ K 8 4	♦ K Q 7	♦ A 6 3
♣ A J 8 5	♣ 7 3	♣ 9 8 4 2	♣ K Q J

WEST	EAST	WEST	EAST
73.	**73.**	**78.**	**78.**
S. opens 1♥.	S. opens 1♥.	N. opens 1♠.	N. opens 1♠.
♠ K Q 8	♠ 7 6 5	♠ A Q	♠ 7
♥ A Q	♥ 8 4 3	♥ A J 6	♥ K 9 2
♦ 7 6 4 2	♦ A Q	♦ K Q 9 4	♦ J 8 2
♣ A K 9 3	♣ Q 7 5 4 2	♣ 9 5 3 2	♣ K Q J 8 7 4

PLAY HANDS ON OVERCALLS AND DEFENSE

Hand 29: Overcall—Leading Partner's Suit—Creating a Void

Dealer North: Nil vulnerable

NORTH
♠ A K
♥ K 8 6 2
♦ K Q 10 9 3
♣ 10 5

WEST
♠ 10 9 8
♥ 4 3
♦ 8 7 6 5 2
♣ K 7 2

EAST
♠ 6 5 4 3
♥ 9 5
♦ A
♣ A Q J 8 6 3

SOUTH
♠ Q J 7 2
♥ A Q J 10 7
♦ J 4
♣ 9 4

WEST	NORTH	EAST	SOUTH
	1♦	2♣	2♥
Pass	4♥	All pass	

Bidding: East's suit is excellent and warrants the overcall. South's 2♥ shows 10 points or better so that North, worth 17 points in support of hearts, has no trouble raising to 4♥.

Lead: ♣2. Lead bottom from three or four to an honor.

Play: East should take the ♣A, cash the ♦A to create a void and lead a low club. West wins with the ♣K and East ruffs the diamond return. This plan would also work if West's ♣2 lead were a singleton, but if West wrongly leads the ♣K, 4♥ will succeed.

Hand 30: Raising an Overcall—Reading the Lead—Creating a Void

Dealer East: Nil vulnerable

NORTH
♠ 6 5
♥ 2
♦ J 7 6 4 3
♣ J 7 5 4 2

WEST
♠ K J 10 9 3
♥ K 9
♦ 10 5 2
♣ A Q 8

EAST
♠ Q 8 4 2
♥ Q J 10 7
♦ Q 9 8
♣ K 9

SOUTH
♠ A 7
♥ A 8 6 5 4 3
♦ A K
♣ 10 6 3

WEST	NORTH	EAST	SOUTH
		Pass	1♥
1♠	Pass	2♠	All pass

Bidding: As the top limit for an overcall is 16 HCP, East raises only to 2♠. No one has enough to push higher.

Lead: ♥2. It is normal to lead your partner's suit and a singleton is very attractive.

Play: South can see that the lead is a singleton. Only one other heart is missing and with a doubleton, your partner would lead the top card, not the bottom. South cashes ♦A-K (A-then-K to show a doubleton), creating a void, and leads a heart for North to ruff. South ruffs the diamond return and the ♠A is the setting trick.

Hand 31: Raising an Overcall—Third Hand High—Finding a Switch

Dealer South: Nil vulnerable

WEST	NORTH	EAST	SOUTH
			1♥
Pass	2♥	2♠	3♥
3♠	Pass	Pass	Pass

NORTH
♠ 5 2
♥ A 9 3 2
♦ 8 2
♣ J 9 8 6 4

WEST
♠ Q 10 3
♥ 8 5 4
♦ J 10 9 4
♣ K Q 7

EAST
♠ A K J 9 8 4
♥ K
♦ K 7 5
♣ 10 5 3

SOUTH
♠ 7 6
♥ Q J 10 7 6
♦ A Q 6 3
♣ A 2

Bidding: East has enough for 2♠ and South should compete to 3♥. Do not sell out at the two-level if your side has a trump fit. 3♥ would succeed, but West raises partner to 3♠. 3-card support is quite enough to raise an overcall.

Lead: ♥Q. Top of a sequence.

Play: Deducing that East holds the ♥K, North plays the ace. When the ♥K drops, it is futile to continue with hearts. North switches to the ♦8, top from a doubleton. South wins, cashes the second diamond winner, and continues diamonds. North ruffs the third round and the ♣A defeats the contract.

Hand 32: Reading the Lead—Third Hand High—Finding the Switch

Dealer West: Nil vulnerable

WEST	NORTH	EAST	SOUTH
Pass	1♥	2♦	2♥
Pass	4♥	All pass	

NORTH
♠ A K
♥ A 10 9 8 5 2
♦ K 3
♣ K J 10

WEST
♠ 8 7 5 4 3 2
♥ 7 4
♦ A 7 5
♣ 9 4

EAST
♠ Q 6
♥ J
♦ Q J 10 9 6 4
♣ A Q 8 7

SOUTH
♠ J 10 9
♥ K Q 6 3
♦ 8 2
♣ 6 5 3 2

Bidding: East's good suit justifies the 2♦ overcall. West is too weak to raise to 3♦. After receiving support, North re-values to 20 points.

Lead: ♦Q. Top of a sequence.

Play: From the lead, West knows that declarer has the ♦K and so plays the ♦A (third-hand-high). When the ♦K does not fall, West sees there are no more diamond tricks for the defense. If returning your partner's suit is futile, it is usually better to switch. West shifts to the ♣9 (top from a doubleton) and ruffs the third club to defeat 4♥.

Chapter 11
Takeout Doubles

If the opponents have opened the bidding and you have a strong hand, you will want to enter the bidding. Yet if you lack a long suit to overcall and the hand is not suitable for a 1NT overcall, you should pass unless your hand meets *all* the requirements for a takeout double. Two basic types of doubles are commonly used: The Penalty Double *which asks your partner to pass* (and aims to collect larger penalties by defeating the opponents' contract) and the Takeout Double *which asks your partner to bid* (and aims to find a decent contract for your side). It is clearly vital to know when your partner's double is for takeout and when it is for penalties.

In traditional methods, a double is for penalties if:
- it is a double of a no-trump bid, *or*
- it is a double at the three-level or higher.

Some partnerships change these conditions, but unless you and your partner have some specific agreement to the contrary, a double under either of the above conditions is intended as a penalty double.

The general rule is that a double is for takeout if it is a double of a suit bid at the one-level or the two-level. A takeout double is usually made at the first opportunity, but this need not be so. It is certainly possible to open the bidding and make a takeout double on the second round, or make an overcall initially and a takeout double on the next round, provided that the above conditions for a takeout double are met. Many partnerships play that a double of a pre-emptive opening at the three-level is also for takeout.

What You Need to Make a Takeout Double

A takeout double has point count requirements *and* shape requirements. The more strength, the more you may depart from the requirements of shape, but for a minimum strength double, the shape factors are vital.

When valuing your hand for a takeout double, count high card points and add 3-2-1 points for a shortage in the opposition's suit: 3 for a void, 2 for a singleton, and 1 for a doubleton. If your hand now measures 13 points or better, you have the minimum strength needed for a double.

The shape requirements for a minimum takeout double are a shortage in the enemy suit (doubleton or shorter) plus support (four cards) in each unbid suit. It is permissible to have tolerance (three cards) in one of the unbid suits. Thus, if your partner doubles a major, expect your partner to have four cards in the other major. If your partner doubles a minor suit, expect at least 4-3 in the major suits. Holding both majors, double with 4-4, 5-4, or 5-5 in the majors but prefer to overcall with 5-3 in the majors when the 5-card suit is strong.

If the opponents have bid two suits, a takeout double shows support for both unbid suits. If the doubler is a passed hand, the takeout double shows 9—11 HCP plus support for any unbid suit. With 16+ HCP, the shape requirements are eased: the doubler need not have a shortage in the enemy suit and need have only tolerance in the unbid suits rather than support. With 19+ HCP, there are no shape requirements for the double.

Responding to Your Partner's Takeout Double

You are expected to answer your partner's takeout double no matter how weak your hand is. The only time you might elect to pass a takeout double, and thus convert it to a penalty double, is when you have better trumps in your hand than the opponent who bid that suit. (Normally, you would need at least five trumps including three honors to pass out a takeout double.) For practical purposes, take your partner's takeout double as forcing.

If you intend to bid a suit in answer to the double, count your HCP and add 5-3-1 ruffing points (5 for a void, 3 for a singleton, 1 for a doubleton). If you intend to bid no-trumps, count only your high card points. After you have assessed the value of your hand, these are your options:

0–5 points:	Bid a suit at the cheapest possible level.
6–9 points:	Bid a suit at the cheapest possible level, or bid 1NT.
10–12 points:	Make a jump-bid in a suit or bid 2NT.
13 points or more:	Bid a game, or bid the enemy suit to force to game.

A suit response thus has a range of 0–9 points (including points for distribution). With the upper end of this range (6–9), try to bid a second time if a convenient opportunity arises. If third player bids over your partner's takeout double, and thus removes it, the obligation to reply to the double ceases. In such a case you should pass with the 0–5 points and make your normal reply with 6 points or more. When responding to a takeout double, ask yourself first, "What shall I bid?" and after you have the answer to that, ask, "How high shall I bid it?"

The order of priority when responding to a takeout double is:

(1) **Bid a major first.** Prefer a major suit to a longer or better minor.

(2) **With no major available, choose a response in no-trumps if possible.** For a no-trumps response, you need at least one stopper in the enemy suit and some high card strength (6–9 points for 1NT). When you hold just 0–5 points, choose a suit bid. The 1NT response is not rubbish.

(3) **If unable to bid a major or no-trumps, bid a minor.**

Rebids by the Doubler

(a) **After a reply showing up to 9 points:** Revalue the hand if a trump fit is located, adding the 5-3-1 ruffing count to the HCP. Then with 13–16 points, pass. With 17–19 points, bid again, and with 20–22 points make a jump-rebid. If the doubler bids again, partner should keep bidding with the 6–9 point hand and pass with 0–5, while if the doubler has made a jump rebid, partner should bid to game if holding one sure trick.

(b) After a response showing 10–12 points: Pass with just 12–13 points, but bid on with 14 points or more and head for a game with 16 or more.

(c) A second bid by the doubler is always a strong action, showing at least 16 points. A change of suit by the doubler shows a 5+ suit and denies support for the suit bid by partner. A rebid in no-trumps by the doubler shows 19–21 points and a balanced hand (since with 1♣–1♠ balanced, you would make an immediate overcall of 1NT, and with 13–15 you should not bid again after doubling if your partner has shown fewer than 10 points). A new suit by the doubler is not forcing if partner has shown 0–9 points, but is forcing if partner made a reply showing 10–12 points.

ACTION BY THIRD HAND AFTER A TAKEOUT DOUBLE

After your partner has opened and the second player doubles, the third player passes with a weak hand, makes a normal bid with 6 points or better and can redouble with 10+ HCP, and no fit for opener's suit. After the redouble, the partner of the doubler should make the normal reply (as the redouble has not removed the double) and the opener should usually pass, unless the hand is suitable to double the last bid for penalties. The redouble promises another bid so that the opener can pass in safety, even with a good hand, knowing that the redoubler will bid again. After a redouble, any double by the opener or the redoubler is a penalty double. The function of the redouble is to confirm that your side has more points than they do and so you can capitalise on the jeopardy in which the opponents find themselves.

EXERCISES ON TAKEOUT DOUBLES

A. In the following auctions, is West's double for takeout or for penalties?

1.	N	E	S	W	2.	N	E	S	W	3.	N	E	S	W
	No	No	1♥	Dble		1♦	No	1♠	Dble		1♥	No	2♥	Dble

4.	N	E	S	W	5.	N	E	S	W	6.	N	E	S	W
	No	1♥	4♠	Dble			No	1NT	Dble		1NT	2♠	Dble	

B. You are East. North opens 1♣. What action do you take on these hands?

1.	♠ K 8 4 3	2.	♠ A J 8 7	3.	♠ A Q 8 7
	♥ Q J 4 2		♥ Q 9 4 3		♥ 6
	♦ A Q 7 2		♦ A 10 7 4 3		♦ A K 10 4 3 2
	♣ 5		♣ - - -		♣ 6 2

4.	♠ A K J 4	5.	♠ A Q J 9 6 5	6.	♠ A Q 8 7 5
	♥ A J 9 6 3		♥ K Q J		♥ 6
	♦ K 2		♦ A K		♦ A K 10 4 3
	♣ 7 4		♣ 5 2		♣ 4 3

7.	♠ A J 9 7	8.	♠ A J 6 2	9.	♠ A 7
	♥ K Q 9		♥ K Q 7		♥ K J 2
	♦ A 8 4 3		♦ J 9 6		♦ A Q J 5
	♣ 6 3		♣ A Q 5		♣ K Q 3 2

C. You are East. North opens 1♥. What action do you take on these hands?

1.	♠ K J 7	2.	♠ K Q	3.	♠ K Q 7 2
	♥ A 8		♥ A 4 3		♥ A 3
	♦ Q 4 3 2		♦ A 8 3 2		♦ A 8 3 2
	♣ Q 9 6 3		♣ J 7 5 4		♣ J 7 5

4. ♠ A K 10 9 6   5. ♠ J 8 3 2   6. ♠ K
    ♥ 3   ♥ 6   ♥ A K 10 9 6 2
    ♦ A 5 4   ♦ A K 7 6 2   ♦ A 7 4
    ♣ Q 8 6 3   ♣ K Q 9   ♣ J 4 3

7. ♠ A Q   8. ♠ A Q   9. ♠ A Q J 6 2
    ♥ K 9 3   ♥ K 9 3   ♥ A 4
    ♦ A J 4 3   ♦ A K 4 3   ♦ A K J 5
    ♣ K 8 7 4   ♣ K J 7 4   ♣ Q 3

D. N   E   S   W   The bidding has started as on the left.

    1♦ **Dble No** ?   What action should West take on these hands?

1. ♠ K 9 7 3   2. ♠ 9 7 3 2   3. ♠ Q 9 8 7 4
    ♥ Q 5   ♥ 8 4 2   ♥ Q 8 6 5
    ♦ 7 6 4 3   ♦ 7 6   ♦ 4 3
    ♣ 8 3 2   ♣ 9 6 4 2   ♣ 6 2

4. ♠ 6 2   5. ♠ A 7 6   6. ♠ 7 6 4
    ♥ Q 8 6 5   ♥ 9 2   ♥ 5 4 3
    ♦ 4 3   ♦ 4 3 2   ♦ 7 6 4 3 2
    ♣ Q 9 8 7 4   ♣ J 9 8 6 3   ♣ 3 2

E. N   E   S   W   The bidding has started as on the left.

    1♣ **Dble No** ?   What action should West take on these hands?

1. ♠ K 9 8 4 3   2. ♠ K 9 5 4   3. ♠ 7 6
    ♥ 6   ♥ A J 10 7 5   ♥ K 8 4
    ♦ 6 4 2   ♦ 4 3   ♦ A Q J 4 2
    ♣ A 7 4 2   ♣ 6 2   ♣ 6 5 3

4. ♠ J 8 4   5. ♠ 8 5   6. ♠ K Q 8 7 4 3
    ♥ A 7 3   ♥ A 7 2   ♥ A 8
    ♦ 8 5 3 2   ♦ A J 9 3   ♦ 2
    ♣ Q J 5   ♣ Q 10 8 7   ♣ 7 6 4 3

F. **N** **E** **S** **W**   The bidding has started as on the left.

1♦ Dble 1♠ ?   What action should West take on these hands?

1. ♠ Q 7   2. ♠ 7 2   3. ♠ 9
    ♥ Q 8 4 3   ♥ Q J 8 4   ♥ A J 9 8 5
    ♦ 9 6 2   ♦ 8 6 5   ♦ 7 6 2
    ♣ 8 6 5 2   ♣ K J 8 7   ♣ K 8 7 2

G. **N** **E** **S** **W**

No No 1♦ Dble   The bidding has started as on the left.

No 1♥ No ?   What action should West take on these hands?

1. ♠ A J 7 4   2. ♠ A J 7 4   3. ♠ A 8 2
    ♥ K Q 4 2   ♥ K Q 4 2   ♥ A K Q 3
    ♦ 7 6   ♦ 7 6   ♦ K Q 9 8 2
    ♣ K 8 2   ♣ A K 3   ♣ 6

PARTNERSHIP BIDDING PRACTICE FEATURING TAKEOUT DOUBLES

There is no North-South bidding other than that shown.

WEST	EAST	WEST	EAST
79.	**79.**	**84.**	**84.**
N. opens 1♥.	N. opens 1♥.	N. opens 1♥.	N. opens 1♥.
♠ J 7	♠ K Q 4 3	♠ K J 7	♠ A Q 9 3
♥ 8 6 4 2	♥ 7	♥ A J 10	♥ 7 2
♦ Q 7 5 3	♦ A J 8 6	♦ 7 6 3	♦ A 9 2
♣ 10 6 5	♣ Q 9 8 3	♣ 8 7 4 2	♣ A Q J 5
80.	**80.**	**85.**	**85.**
S. opens 1♥.	S. opens 1♥.	S. opens 1♠.	S. opens 1♠.
♠ A K 7 6	♠ 10 8 4	♠ 7	♠ A 8 5 2
♥ 8 3	♥ 9 7 6	♥ A Q 8 3	♥ J 10 2
♦ A Q 9	♦ 4 3	♦ K Q 9 3	♦ A 7 4
♣ J 7 6 4	♣ K 9 5 3 2	♣ A J 9 2	♣ Q 8 3
81.	**81.**	**86.**	**86.**
S. opens 1♣.	S. opens 1♣.	S. opens 1♥.	S. opens 1♥.
♠ A K J 6	♠ Q 9 4 3	♠ A 8 6 2	♠ K Q 9 7 5
♥ K Q J 4	♥ 8 7	♥ 7 4	♥ A 2
♦ A 4 3	♦ 9 8 5 2	♦ A K 6 2	♦ 7 4 3
♣ 9 2	♣ 8 7 6	♣ J 8 5	♣ 9 6 3
82.	**82.**	**87.**	**87.**
N. opens 1♣.	N. opens 1♣.	N. opens 1♣.	N. opens 1♣.
♠ 9 7	♠ A K 5 2	♠ K Q J 6 5 2	♠ A 7 4 3
♥ 6 5 4 2	♥ K Q J 7 3	♥ 7 5	♥ A 9 8 2
♦ 7 6 4	♦ K Q	♦ K J	♦ A 5 4 3
♣ J 8 3 2	♣ 9 7	♣ Q 6 2	♣ 7
83.	**83.**	**88.**	**88.**
N. opens 1♦.	N. opens 1♦.	S. opens 1♦.	S. opens 1♦.
♠ K Q 8 7	♠ A 9 6 3	♠ A K J 7	♠ 6 4
♥ 7 6	♥ K Q 8 5	♥ A 10 9 6 2	♥ K 8 3
♦ 5 4	♦ 9 6	♦ 9	♦ J 6 5
♣ 8 6 4 3 2	♣ A 7 5	♣ A 6 2	♣ K Q J 8 3

PLAY HANDS ON TAKEOUT DOUBLES

Hand 33: Leading towards Honor Cards When Two Honors Are Missing

Dealer North: Nil vulnerable

NORTH
♠ J 10 8 7 4 3
♥ 6
♦ 10 9 5
♣ J 5 3

WEST
♠ K Q 6 5
♥ K Q 5 4
♦ A J 6 4
♣ 4

EAST
♠ A 2
♥ 9 8 7 3 2
♦ K 3
♣ Q 10 6 2

SOUTH
♠ 9
♥ A J 10
♦ Q 8 7 2
♣ A K 9 8 7

WEST	NORTH	EAST	SOUTH
	Pass	Pass	1♣
Double	Pass	2♥	Pass
4♥	Pass	Pass	Pass

Bidding: East's 2♥ jump reply to the double shows 10–12 points.

Lead: ♣A. Normal from A-K suits.

Play: South switches to the ♠9. East wins in hand and leads a heart to the K, which wins. As South is marked with the ♥A, do not lead a second heart from dummy. A diamond goes to the king and another heart is led *towards* dummy. This holds the defense to just one trump trick. One club loser can be ruffed later and another goes on the third spade.

Hand 34: Delaying Trumps to Take a Quick Discard

Dealer East: E-W vulnerable

NORTH
♠ 8
♥ K J 10 6 5 4
♦ A 6
♣ J 9 6 2

WEST
♠ Q 9 7 2
♥ 7
♦ 10 9 7 3
♣ 10 8 5 3

EAST
♠ J 5 4 3
♥ A Q 2
♦ K Q J 8 4
♣ Q

SOUTH
♠ A K 10 6
♥ 9 8 3
♦ 5 2
♣ A K 7 4

WEST	NORTH	EAST	SOUTH
		1♦	Double
Pass	4♥	All pass	

Bidding: North is worth 13 points (3 for the singleton and 1 for the doubleton). With 13 points or more opposite a takeout double, you should reach some game. 4♥ is the clear choice.

Lead: ♦K. Prefer the sequence.

Play: Win ♦A, play the ♠A and ♠K to discard the diamond loser. Then lead a trump, finessing the jack. Declarer should keep on with trumps until all are drawn. West should hold on to the clubs ("keep length with dummy"). When East shows out on the second club, North finesses the ♣9 if necessary.

Hand 35: Signalling with a Doubleton—Card Reading by Declarer
Dealer South: Both vulnerable

WEST	NORTH	EAST	SOUTH
			Pass
1♦	Double	Pass	1♥
Pass	2♥	All pass	

```
              NORTH
              ♠ A K Q J
              ♥ K 7 5 3
              ♦ K
              ♣ Q 4 3 2
WEST                          EAST
♠ 8 5                         ♠ 10 9 7 4 2
♥ Q 9                         ♥ 10 8 6
♦ Q J 7 5 2                   ♦ A 10 3
♣ A K J 8                     ♣ 9 5
              SOUTH
              ♠ 6 3
              ♥ A J 4 2
              ♦ 9 8 6 4
              ♣ 10 7 6
```

Bidding: Opposite 0–9 points, North is worth a mild try for game and raises to 2♥, but South is too weak to bid on.

Lead: ♣A. A-K leads are attractive.

Play: East signals with the ♣9 to encourage a club continuation and ruffs a third round of clubs. East cashes the ♦A and exits with a diamond or a spade. With only 17 HCP missing and the ♦A with East, the ♥Q is marked with West. South rejects the normal finesse for the queen when holding eight trumps and plays the ♥K and ♥A. The ♥Q drops, lucky—9 tricks.

Hand 36: Card Reading—Finessing—Careful Use of Entries
Dealer West: Both vulnerable

WEST	NORTH	EAST	SOUTH
Pass	1♠	Double	Pass
2NT	Pass	3NT	All pass

```
              NORTH
              ♠ K Q J 10 7
              ♥ K 8 6 2
              ♦ 9 4
              ♣ A 10
WEST                          EAST
♠ A 9 3 2                     ♠ 5
♥ 7 4 3                       ♥ A Q J 10
♦ K J 8                       ♦ A Q 5 2
♣ Q J 5                       ♣ K 8 7 2
              SOUTH
              ♠ 8 6 4
              ♥ 9 5
              ♦ 10 7 6 3
              ♣ 9 6 4 3
```

Bidding: 2NT denies four hearts and shows 10–12 points, balanced, with at least one stopper in spades. East has enough to try for game and 3NT looks the best bet.

Lead: ♠K, to set up the spades.

Play: After taking the ♠A, West should realize that it is futile to go for clubs. North will win and cash the rest of the spades. As only 13 HCP are missing, North must have the ♥K for the opening bid. So, finesse ♥Q, diamond to the jack, finesse ♥J, diamond to the king, finesse ♥10, and you have nine tricks.

Chapter 12
Penalty Doubles

When you are confident that you can defeat the opponents' contract, it is highly attractive to double them. The bonus points for penalties mount up quickly if you beat them by more than one trick. If they are not vulnerable, you collect 50 points for every trick by which they fail, but if you have doubled them, you collect 100 for one down, 300 for two down, 500 for three down, and 300 for each additional trick. If they are vulnerable, it is even more lucrative. Undoubled, they lose only 100 per trick. Doubled, they lose 200 for one down and 300 for each additional trick. Three down, doubled, not vulnerable, or two down, doubled, and vulnerable equals 500, as much as completing the rubber by two games to one.

On the other hand, if they make their contract doubled, they score double points, plus 50 for the insult of being doubled. Overtricks made when doubled are more valuable than usual: 100 points per overtrick when not vulnerable and 200 points per overtrick when vulnerable. Consider also that if they redouble and make it, the preceding scores are doubled again. Therefore, be fairly sure you can defeat them before you double.

When to Double Their 1NT Opening

You should hold at least as many points as they do. Double a strong 1NT with 17+ HCP. Double a weak 1NT (12–14 or 13–15 HCP) if holding 15+ HCP. Your partner is expected to pass your double, but with a woeful hand and a long suit, your partner is permitted to remove your double and bid the long suit. Remove a penalty double only with a very weak hand. If either opponent bids a suit after their 1NT has been doubled, you or your partner should double this with a strong 4-card or better holding in that suit.

When to Double Their 1NT Overcall

When your partner has opened and second player overcalls 1NT, double if your side has more points than they do. If they are trying for more than half the tricks with less than half the points, they will usually fail. Therefore, to maximize your score, double their 1NT overcall whenever you hold 9 HCP or better. Again, after their 1NT has been doubled, if either opponent tries to escape by bidding a suit, you or your partner should double this rescue attempt with a strong 4-card holding in that suit.

When to Double Their Suit Overcall at the 1-level

To extract a decent penalty at the 1-level, you need excellent trumps. To defeat them at all, you have to take seven tricks. This is equivalent to making a contract of one or more in their suit with a known bad break. Consequently, your trumps should be better than theirs and the minimum recommended is five trumps with three honors. It is also helpful to have a shortage in the suit your partner opened and at least 20 HCP for your side.

When to Double Their Suit Overcall at the 2-level

The requirements are slightly less but you still should be strong in their trump suit. For a double at the 2-level you should hold:
- At least 20 HCP between you and your partner, *and*
- Four or more trumps, including at least two honors, *and*
- A shortage in your partner's suit, preferably a singleton.

When to Double Their Suit at the 3-level

As doubles above 2♦ give them a game if they succeed, you need to be very confident you will defeat them. For a penalty double at the 3-level you should have six or more tricks between you and your partner, including at least one trump trick. Your partner should hold 1-2 tricks with 6–10 HCP and 2-3 tricks with 11–15 HCP. Add your own winners to this expectancy.

If you are highly likely to make a game, do not settle for a small penalty; rather bid on to your best game. If you can make a game, you need at least 500 points from the double as compensation for the game missed.

When to Double Their Game Contracts

If they bid above your game, double if your side has more points, but otherwise it usually does not pay to double their game, even though you hope to beat it. Points are not enough. Your expected winners might be ruffed. The best time to double is if they have barely enough for game (after an invitational auction like 1♥: 1NT, 2♦: 2♥, 3♥: 4♥) *and* you know they are in for a bad break in trumps. Double and collect big.

When to Double Their Slams

Almost never double. You might collect an extra 50 or 100 but they collect an extra 230 (or 640 if they redouble) if they make it. Even with Q-J-10-9 in trumps, pass and be satisfied to defeat them. If you double, they might bid some other slam, such as 6NT, which you cannot beat. What a disaster!

Appendix 1:

From Whist to Bridge

The following games provide a suitable introduction to those who have never played bridge before.

What Type of Game Is Bridge?

There are two basic families of card games. In one, the aim is to form combinations of cards, such as Gin Rummy and Canasta. Contract Bridge belongs to the other in which the aim is to win tricks. Other games in the trick-taking family are Solo, Five Hundred, Whist, and Euchre.

Bridge is played by four people, two playing as partners against the other two. Partners sit opposite each other. You will need a card table, four chairs, preferably two packs of cards (though you can manage with one pack), score pads, and pencils.

How Many Cards Are in the Pack?

A pack (or deck) of 52 cards is used. There are no jokers. There are four suits: spades ♠, hearts ♥, diamonds ♦, and clubs ♣. Each suit has thirteen cards, the highest being the ace followed by the king, queen, jack, 10, 9, 8, 7, 6, 5, 4, 3, and down to the 2, which is the lowest.

How Do We Choose Partners?

You may agree to play in certain partnerships, but it is usual to draw for partners. Spread out one pack, face down, and each player picks a card. The two who draw the higher cards play as partners against the other two, normally for one or two "rubbers." Then, cards are drawn again to form two new partnerships. If two or more cards of the same rank are turned up, then the tie is split according to suit, the suits ranking from the highest, spades, through hearts and diamonds, to the lowest, clubs.

Who Deals?

The player who drew the highest card has the right to choose seats and which pack of cards to use for dealing, and also becomes the dealer on the first hand. The next dealer will be the player on the left of the previous dealer and so on in clockwise rotation. The cards are shuffled by the player on the dealer's left who passes them across the table to the player on the dealer's right to "cut" them. The dealer completes the "cut" and then deals the cards, one at a time, face down in clockwise direction, starting with the player on the dealer's left, until all 52 cards are dealt.

It is customary etiquette not to pick up your cards until the dealer has finished dealing. This allows the dealer equal time to study the cards and also allows a misdeal to be corrected. During the deal, the dealer's partner is shuffling the other pack in preparation for the next deal. Using two packs speeds up the game. After the shuffling is complete, the cards are placed on the shuffler's right, ready for the next dealer to pick up.

THE START OF PLAY

After picking up your thirteen cards, sort them into suits. It is usual to separate the red suits and the black suits and also to put your cards in order of rank in each suit. The bidding starts with the dealer. More about the bidding later.

GAME 1—WHIST

Each player receives thirteen cards. Opposite players are partners. There is no bidding yet. The top card of the other pack is turned face up. If it is a 2, 3, or 4, the hand is to be played in no-trumps. If it is a

5 or higher, the suit of the faced card will be trumps for that deal. The player on the left of the dealer makes the first lead—that is, places one card face up on the table. Each player in turn, in clockwise order, plays a card face up. That group of four cards, one from each player, is called a "trick." *Each player must follow suit if possible.* If unable to follow suit at no-trumps, discard those cards that you judge to be worthless. When there is a trump suit, you are permitted to play a trump card, which beats any card in any other suit.

A trick with no trump card is won by the highest card in the suit led. A trick with a trump card is won by the highest trump card on the trick. You may play a high card or a low card but, if possible, you must follow suit. One situation where you could win the trick, but it could be foolish to do so, is if your partner's card has already won the trick.

Play continues until all thirteen tricks have been played. Each side then counts up the number of tricks won. The side winning more than six tricks is the winner and is the only side that scores points.

SCORING

The first partnership to score **100 points or more** in tricks won scores a **Game**. We play a **Rubber** of bridge. A rubber is **the best of three games**. Game 1 is worth +350. Game 2 is worth +350. A rubber ends when one side wins two games. If a third game is needed, Game 3 is worth +500.

Scoring—No-Trumps
30 points for each trick won over six, plus 10.

Scoring—Trumps
With Spades or Hearts as trumps: 30 points for each trick over six. With Diamonds or Clubs as trumps: 20 points for each trick over six.

A bridge scoresheet consists of two columns with a vertical line down the middle. It also has a horizontal line across both columns a little more than halfway down the columns. It thus looks like an inverted cross.

Trick scores are written below the horizontal line, bonus scores above it. Your scores go in the left-hand column, theirs in the right-hand column. At the end of a game, a line is ruled across both columns below the tricks score and both sides start the next game from zero again.

At the end of a rubber, both columns are totalled. The side scoring more points is the winner. The difference between the two scores is rounded to the nearest 100 (a difference ending in 50 is rounded down). The score is then entered as the number of 100s won or lost. For example, if you won by 930, your scoresheet reads: "+9" while theirs would record "-9."

GUIDELINES FOR PLAY AT NO-TRUMPS

Prefer to lead your longest suit and keep leading it. When the others run out, your remaining cards in that suit will be winners. As players lead their own long suit, prefer to return your partner's led suit, unless you have a strong suit of your own. Usually avoid returning a suit led by the opposition.

Second player to a trick commonly plays low; third player normally plays high. If your partner's card has already won the trick, you need not play high.

The card to lead: Top card from a sequence of 3 or more cards headed by the ten or higher (from K-Q-J-5, lead the K; from J-10-9-2, lead the J).

Lead fourth-highest (fourth from the top) when the long suit has no three-card or longer sequence (from K-J-8-6-3, lead the 6).

GUIDELINES FOR PLAY AT TRUMPS

Leading the longest suit is not so attractive. Prefer to lead a strong suit (headed by a sequence or by A-K) or a singleton (so you can ruff). With plenty of trumps, lead trumps to remove the opponents' trump cards so that they cannot ruff your winners. If you decide to lead a doubleton (a two-card suit), standard technique is to lead top card.

After a few of these games, move on to Game 2.

GAME 2—DUMMY WHIST

Each player receives thirteen cards and counts the high card points (HCP), using A = 4, K = 3, Q = 2, and J = 1. Starting with the dealer, each player calls out the total number of points held. The side which has more points becomes the declarer side and the partner that has more points becomes the declarer. (The pack has 40 HCP. If each side has 20, re-deal the hand. For a tie within the declarer side, the player nearer the dealer is to be the declarer.)

The declarer's partner is known as the "dummy." The dummy hand is placed face up on the table, neatly in suits facing declarer. The declarer then nominates the trump suit or no-trumps. Choose a trump suit with 8+ cards in the two hands. With more than one trump suit available, choose a major (spades or hearts) rather than a minor (diamonds or clubs). The majors score more. With two majors or two minors, choose the longer. With equal length, choose the stronger. With no suit of 8+ trumps together, play no-trumps.

After the trump suit or no-trumps has been declared, the player on the left of the declarer makes the first lead. The play proceeds as before but **the declarer must play both hands.** The dummy player takes no part in the play. If dummy wins a trick, the next lead comes from dummy, while if declarer wins a trick, declarer must lead to the next trick.

SCORING

If declarer scores 7+ tricks, scoring is as usual. If declarer fails to win 7 tricks, the opponents score bonus points. Only the declarer side score points for game. If the declarer side has not won a game ("not vulnerable"), the opponents score 50 points for each trick by which they have defeated declarer, regardless of the trump suit or whether no-trumps is played. Where the declarer side has won one game ("vulnerable"), the opponents score 100 points for each trick by which they defeated declarer.

Bonus Points, scored above the line, do not count towards a game. They are valuable since they count in your total points at the end of the rubber. The existence of the dummy sets bridge apart from other trick-taking games. From the first lead, each player sees half the pack (13 cards in hand and the 13 cards in dummy), thus making Bridge essentially a game of skill in contrast to other games, which have a large luck factor. Since the declarer side in this game will have more points than the defenders, the declarer side is more likely to succeed in taking seven or more tricks.

After a few of these games, move on to Game 3.

GAME 3—BIDDING WHIST

Starting with the dealer, each player states the number of points held. The side with more points is the declarer side and the two partners discuss which suit shall be trumps or whether to play no-trumps. Each partner in turn suggests a trump suit or no-trumps, until agreement is reached. This is known as the "bidding" or the "auction." A bid is just a suggestion to your partner which suit you prefer as trumps or whether you prefer no-trumps.

A suggested trump suit must contain at least four cards. With no long suit and with no void or singleton it is often best to suggest no-trumps at once. If there is no early agreement and neither partner insists on a suit, one of the partners should suggest no-trumps. After agreement, the first player to suggest the agreed trump suit (or no-trumps, if agreed) is the declarer.

The player on the left of the declarer makes the opening lead *before seeing dummy.* After the lead, dummy's 13 cards are placed face up (in suits) facing declarer (trumps on dummy's right). The scoring is the same as for Game 2.

GAME 4—CONTRACT WHIST

Proceed as for Game 3 above, but declarer is required to win a specific number of tricks depending on the total points held by declarer and dummy:

20–22 points:	7 or more tricks in no-trumps
	8 or more tricks with a trump suit
23–25 points:	8 or more tricks in no-trumps
	9 or more tricks with a trump suit
26–32 points:	9 or more tricks in no-trumps
	10 or more tricks with ♥ or ♠ as trumps
	11 or more tricks with ♣ or ♦ as trumps
33–36 points:	12 or more tricks
37–40 points:	All 13 tricks

PLAY: The opening lead is made before dummy is tabled.

SCORING: As for Game 2, but declarer must win the number of tricks stipulated or more. If not, the defenders score 50 (declarer not vulnerable) or 100 (declarer vulnerable) for each trick by which declarer fails.

If required to win twelve tricks, the declarer side (if successful) scores an extra 500 not vulnerable, 750 vulnerable. If required to win all thirteen tricks, the declarer side (if successful) scores an extra 1,000 not vulnerable, 1,500 vulnerable.

If extra time is available, more games similar to these can be played.

Appendix 2:

The Stayman Convention

All experienced players understand the Stayman 2♣ Convention to locate the best game contract in a major suit in preference to no-trumps. When you have been playing for some time, you will want to include Stayman in your system, since it is part and parcel of all standard systems.

The 2♣ response to 1NT asks your partner, "Do you have a 4-card major?" If opener has a major, opener bids it (bidding 2♥ if opener has two 4-card majors). The negative reply, denying a 4-card major, is 2♦.

WHEN TO USE STAYMAN

Use the 2♣ reply to 1NT when you hold:
- 8+ HCP, *and*
- One 4-card major or both majors, 4-4, 5-4, or 5-5

Replies to 2♣ Stayman
- 2♦ = No major suit
- 2♥ = 4 hearts (may have spades also)
- 2♠ = 4 spades (will not have four hearts)

AFTER OPENER'S REPLY TO STAYMAN

A new suit by responder is a 5-card suit and a jump-bid is forcing to game (e.g., 1NT: 2♣, 2♦: 3♠ would show five spades and enough for game). If opener has bid one major, a bid of no-trumps by responder would show that responder had four cards in the other major. Responder's rebid of 2NT invites game (like 1NT: 2NT immediately).

Raising opener's major suit to the 3-level likewise invites game and shows support for opener's major.

STAYMAN WITH WEAK RESPONDING HANDS

When responder bids 2♣ over 1NT and rebids 3♣ over opener's answer, responder is showing six or more clubs and a very weak hand (not enough for a game). Opener is expected to pass. Responder's rebid of 2-in-a-major is also a weak rebid showing a 5-card suit. Opener would normally pass but may raise the major with 3-card support and a maximum 1NT opening.

STAYMAN OVER A 2NT OPENING

The 3♣ response to a 2NT opening operates in the same way as Stayman over 1NT, except that opener's replies occur at the 3-level. To use Stayman over 2NT, responder should have enough strength for game and either one 4-card major or both majors. A new suit rebid by responder after the reply to Stayman would show at least a 5-card suit and would be forcing.

Appendix 3:
Opening Leads—The Suit to Lead

AGAINST NO-TRUMP CONTRACTS

Under normal circumstances, the best strategy is to lead your longest suit. Both defenders should continue with that suit at every opportunity unless the play of the hand clearly indicates it is futile to do so:

- Lead your own longest suit, *but*
- Prefer to lead a long suit bid by your partner, *and*
- Avoid leading a suit shown by the opponents.

Where your partner has not bid a suit and your long suit has been bid by the opponents, choose another long suit if you have one. If not, be prepared to lead even a 3-card suit. When faced with this decision to lead a short suit, prefer a major to a minor, longer to shorter and stronger to weaker.

AGAINST TRUMP CONTRACTS

Now it is not so attractive to lead your long suit, since declarer or dummy is likely to ruff it after one or two rounds. Prefer one of these strong leads:

- A suit headed by a solid sequence, such as K-Q-J, Q-J-l0, J-10-9, etc.
- A suit headed by A-K-Q or A-K, *or*
- A singleton, *or*
- A suit bid by your partner.

If none of the above attractive leads exists:

- Lead a suit with two honors rather than a suit with just one honor.
- Lead a doubleton rather than a suit with just one honor.
- Lead a suit with no honors rather than a suit with just one honor.
- Lead a trump from two or three worthless trumps if there is no evidence from the bidding that dummy holds a long suit.
- Lead an unbid suit if dummy is known to hold a long suit. With just one honor card in the possible suits to lead, prefer a suit with the king to one with the queen; prefer a suit with the queen to one with the jack; prefer a suit with the jack to one with just the ace.
- If you hold four or more trumps, lead your longest suit outside trumps to try to force declarer to ruff and so reduce declarer's trump length.

Avoid these dreadful leads:

- A suit headed by the ace without the king as well, *or*
- Doubleton honors, such as K-x, Q-x, J-x (unless your partner bid the suit), *or*
- A singleton trump, *or*
- A suit bid by the opposition.

Appendix 4:

Opening Leads—The Card to Lead

Top from a doubleton.

From three cards: Top of two or three touching cards headed by an honor; bottom with one honor or non-touching honors; middle with no honor (then the top card, then lowest, Middle-Up-Down, MUD).

From four or more cards: Top from solid sequences or near sequences or from touching honors if holding three honors; fourth-highest otherwise.

In the list below, the card to lead is the same whether you are leading your partner's suit or your own. The recommended leads are for trump contracts. The same apply for no-trump contracts except for those with an asterisk.

Holding	Lead	Holding	Lead	Holding	Lead
9 5	9	Q J 10 2	Q	A K	K
9 5 3	5	Q J 9 2	Q	A 6	A
9 6 5 3 2	3	Q J 8 2	2	A K Q	A
10 9	10	Q 10 9 8	10	A K J	A
10 6	10	Q 10 8 3	3	A K 3	A
10 9 3	10	Q 9 8 7 6	7	A 9 3**	A
10 6 3	3	Q 8 6 5 2	5	A K Q 3	A
10 6 3 2	2	K Q	K	A K J 3	A
10 9 8 3	10	K 2	K	A K 6 3*	A
10 9 7 3	10	K Q 5	K	A Q J 3***	A

Holding	Lead	Holding	Lead	Holding	Lead
10 9 6 3	3	K J 10	J	A Q 6 3*	A
J 10	J	K J 5	5	A J 10 3***	A
J 5	J	K 10 9	10	A J 6 3*	A
J 10 6	J	K 10 5	5	A 10 9 8***	A
J 5 2	2	K 7 5	5	A 10 5 2*	A
J 5 4 2	2	K Q J 2	K	A 9 8 7*	A
J 9 8 7 6	7	K Q 10 2	K	A 9 6 3*	A
J 7 5 4 2	4	K Q 9 2*	K	A K J 4 2	A
J 10 9 4	J	K J 10 2	J	A K 7 4 2*	A
J 10 8 4	J	K J 9 2	2	A Q J 4 2***	A
J 10 7 4	4	K 10 9 8	10	A Q 10 9 2***	A
Q J	Q	K 10 8 4	4	A Q 10 4 2*	A
Q 4	Q	K Q J 6 3	K	A Q 6 4 2*	A
Q J 4	Q	K Q 10 6 3	K	A J 10 5 3***	A
Q 10 9	10	K Q 7 6 3*	K	A J 8 5 3*	A
Q 10 4	4	K 9 8 7 3	7	A 10 9 8 3***	A
Q 6 4	4	K 8 6 4 3	4	A 10 8 5 3*	A

* Lead fourth-highest against no-trumps

** Lead bottom against no-trumps

*** Lead the top of the touching honors against no-trumps, e.g., Q from AQJxx, J from AJ10xx, 10 from A109, A1098, or AQ109x, and so on.

Appendix 5:
Negative Doubles

INTRODUCTION

In former standard methods if your partner had bid, any subsequent double by you was for penalties. Thus, if the bidding had started 1♦ from your partner, an overcall of 1♠ on your right and you doubled, it would mean that you had very strong spades (and 5 or 6 of them) and felt that 1♠ doubled was the best spot for your side.

The negative double is quite a different approach. The definition of the negative double is "a double by responder after partner has opened with a suit bid and second player has made a suit overcall." The negative double is for takeout, not for penalties. This approach has become an integral part of successful competitive bidding.

Without the negative double many hands are difficult to bid sensibly after opposition interference. This is particularly so because of the very strict requirements for a two-level response (at least 10 points). Suppose you pick up ♠ A765 ♥ K642 ♦ 763 ♣ 87 and your partner opens 1♦. You intend to respond 1♥, allowing the partnership to find any available major suit fit. However, when second player overcalls 2♣, you are too weak to respond at the two-level. In standard methods you would have to pass. Obviously a good fit in either major could be lost.

Similarly, if you hold ♠ 76 ♥ K874 ♦ A732 ♣ 852 and the bidding starts 1♣ from your partner, 1♠ on your right, a heart fit might be lost in standard methods. There is no satisfactory response (too weak for 2♥ or 2♦, support too poor for 2♣ and the lack of a stopper negates 1NT).

The Solution

Using responder's double for takeout makes competitive bidding simpler and more efficient. On the first hand above, responder doubles 2♣ for takeout, showing both majors (as a takeout double normally does). If your partner has a fit in either major it will be known at once and your partner bids as high as the cards warrant. On the second hand, responder doubles 1♠, showing four or more hearts (as a takeout double of 1♠ usually does). If your partner also has four hearts, the fit will be discovered at once.

Agree with your partner *in advance* to use negative doubles. Initially, adopt them only after an intervening suit bid at the one-level or two-level. Opener will assume that responder holds 6–9 points (a minimum response). With a better hand, responder will bid again later.

Specific Situations

(a) Minor-Minor: Your partner opens with a minor suit and they overcall in a minor suit, for example, 1♣: (1♦), or 1♦: (2♣), or 1♣: (2♦)… Here a double shows both majors, at least 4-4, perhaps 5-4 or 5-5. A major suit bid at the 1-level need not be longer than 4 cards and promises 6 points or more. A major suit response at the two-level (after a two-level overcall) promises a 5-card or longer suit, 10 points or more and is forcing.

(b) Minor-Major or Major-Minor: If only one major suit has been bid so far, the negative double promises at least 4 cards in the other major. 1♣: (1♠): Double shows at least 4 hearts; 1♥: (2♣): Double shows at least 4 spades. If your partner opens with a minor suit and they intervene with 1♥, the double now promises precisely four spades while a response of 1♠ conveys at least five spades. Major-over-major shows a 5+ suit.

(c) Major-Major: If your partner opens in one major and they intervene with the other major, the double now shows both minors, at least 4-4 but possibly 5-4, 5-5, or 6-4. The negative double would promise 6 points or more, while a change of suit by responder at the two-level or higher would promise 10 points or more. Suppose you pick up a hand like this: ♠43 ♥4 ♦K8754 ♣AJ642 and the bidding starts with 1♠ from your partner and 2♥ on your right. Instead of fearing interference, you would welcome it here if you are using negative doubles, since the double allows you to express the nature and strength of the hand quite accurately. Without the interference you would have no descriptive response.

SUBSEQUENT BIDDING AFTER A NEGATIVE DOUBLE

Where responder's negative double has promised a specific major, opener rebids as though the responder had bid that major at the one-level. For example, if the bidding has started 1♣: (1♠): Double . . . the opener continues as though responder had replied 1♥. Thus, if fourth player passes and opener rebids 3♥, that is equivalent to an auction of 1♣: 1♥, 3♥ without interference.

A negative double followed by a change of suit by responder shows at least a 5-card suit and at most 9 HCP. With 10+ points and a 5-card suit, responder is strong enough to bid the suit at once. For example, if opener starts with 1♣ and responder doubles a 1♠ overcall, and over opener's 2♣ rebid, responder rebids 2♥, responder is showing 5 or more hearts and 6–9 points only. With more, the original response would have been 2♥.

EXAMPLE HANDS USING THE NEGATIVE DOUBLE

How should the following hands be bid? West is the dealer on each hand and North intervenes with 1♠ on each hand. No other opposition bidding.

Hand 1
WEST
♠ 8 4
♥ K 7 6
♦ A 4
♣ A Q 7 4 3 2

Hand 1
EAST
♠ 9 5 2
♥ A J 5 3
♦ J 10 9 3
♣ J 6

After 1♣ West, 1♠ by North, East doubles to show 4 hearts and 6+ points. Unable to support hearts or rebid in no-trumps, West rebids 2♣ to show a minimum opening and a long club suit. With a minimum double, East passes.

Hand 2
WEST
♠ A 4
♥ 6 4
♦ K Q 7 6 5
♣ K J 3 2

Hand 2
EAST
♠ 3 2
♥ Q J 10 9 3 2
♦ 8 4
♣ A 5 4

After 1♦ West, 1♠ by North, East is too weak for 2♥ (10+ points needed) and doubles (only 6+ points, with at least 4 hearts). West rebids 2♣ and East removes to 2♥, confirming 5+ hearts and 6-9 points. West passes.

Hand 3
WEST
♠ A 9 3 2
♥ K 9 8 4
♦ Q
♣ A 6 4 3

Hand 3
EAST
♠ 6 5
♥ A 6 3 2
♦ A J 3 2
♣ K 8 7

After 1♣ West, 1♠ North, East has enough for game, but which game? East doubles and awaits further information. West bids 2♥ (four hearts, but only a minimum opening). East knows now to bid 4♥.

Hand 4
WEST
♠ 7 3
♥ A 8
♦ A 9 8 7 3 2
♣ A 8 6

Hand 4
EAST
♠ A 10
♥ K 9 7 3
♦ K Q 4
♣ J 4 3 2

After 1♦ West, 1♠ North, East has enough for game but should double to try for hearts rather than bid no-trumps at once. When West rebids 2♦ with a minimum opening but not four hearts, East rebids 3NT as there is no heart fit.

Hand 5
WEST
♠ 8
♥ A Q 7 2
♦ K Q 3
♣ A Q J 8 4

Hand 5
EAST
♠ 7 6 2
♥ K 9 5 3
♦ A 7 6 4
♣ 6 5

After 1♣ by West, 1♠ by North, East doubles, showing 4+ hearts and 6+ points). With 3 for the singleton, West is worth 21 points in support of hearts and therefore rebids 4♥. A fringe benefit of negative doubles is that the strong hand is often declarer.

Appendix 6:

Bridge Myths and Fallacies

The following common fallacies may contain a grain of truth or logic but any value vanishes when they are treated as absolute, unfailing universal principles. At best, they are reasonable guides, which should be discarded when the circumstances warrant.

(1) Always lead top of your partner's suit: No, no, a thousand times no. This approach can cost you tricks time after time. Lead top only from a doubleton or from a sequence or from three cards headed by two touching honors, but lead bottom from three or four to an honor. See Appendix 4 and page 131.

(2) Always return your partner's lead: This has more merit but the rule is too wide. It is often best to return your partner's lead but many situations require a switch (see Hands 31 and 32, page 104). Keep in mind the number of tricks needed to defeat the contract. Unless a passive defense is clearly indicated, avoid continuing suits which are known to be futile for beating the contract.

(3) Never lead from a king: To lead from a king-high holding is not an especially attractive lead, but there are far worse combinations. It is usually more dangerous to lead away from a suit headed by the queen or by the jack and far worse in a trump contract to lead from a suit headed by the ace without the king as well. The leads of J-x or Q-x in an unbid suit are also far more dangerous than leading from a king. Leading from a king is acceptable when other choices are even riskier.

(4) Always cover an honor with an honor: Rubbish. It is correct to cover an honor with an honor if it will promote cards in your hand or might promote winners for your partner. In the trump suit in particular, it is usually wrong to cover an honor unless your partner has length in trumps.

(5) Lead through strength, lead up to weakness: This has some sense, but card reading and counting can provide better guides for the defense. Leading through strength does not apply to the opening lead (it is rarely best to lead dummy's bid suit) and in the middle game, the rule refers to short suits (doubletons or tripletons). It is normally not in your best interests to attack dummy's or declarer's long side suit.

(6) Eight ever, nine never: When missing the queen of a long suit, proper technique is to finesse for it if you have 8 cards together, and to play the ace and king, hoping the queen will drop, when you have 9. When playing a complete hand, however, there can be many other considerations.

Appendix 7:

Ethics and Etiquette

Bridge enjoys immense popularity partly because of the high standards of ethics and etiquette, which are observed by the players who are expected to conduct themselves in a highly civilised manner. Violations of proper etiquette are quite common from inexperienced players, either through ignorance or inadvertence. A well-mannered opponent who is the victim of a violation by such a novice player will, if comment is considered necessary, be at pains to make it clear that the comment is intended to be helpful and will never make a newcomer feel ill-at-ease.

Bridge is an extremely ethical game. All good players strive to ensure that their bridge ethics are impeccable and no more serious charge, other than outright cheating, can be made than to accuse a player of bad ethics. Unlike poker in which all sorts of mannerisms, misleading statements, and bluff tactics are part and parcel of the game, bridge is played with a "poker face!" Beginners are, of course, excused for their lapses and in social games nobody minds very much. However, in serious competition your bridge demeanour must be beyond reproach.

When dummy, do not look at either opponent's hand or at declarer's. If you do, you lose your rights as dummy. Do not stand behind declarer to see how you would play. In tournament bridge do not discuss the previous deal if another deal is still to be played. After a deal is over, do not take an opponent's cards and look at them without permission. As a kibitzer (onlooker) try to watch only one hand and, above all, make no facial expressions during a deal. Do not comment or talk during or between deals. If the players want the benefit of your views, they will ask for them.

Conversation at the table in serious games is generally unwelcome. Post-mortems after each hand, if limited, can be useful as long as they seek to be constructive. It is best to keep all post-mortems until the session is over when you can go over the scoresheets with your partner at leisure. During the session, conserve your energies to do battle at the next table. It is extremely poor taste to abuse or criticise your partner or an opponent. Experienced players should go out of their way to make novice players feel at ease, so that they see bridge as a pleasant recreation, not a battleground. Never try to teach anyone at the table. Never let a harsh word pass your lips and you will be a sought-after rather than a shunned partner. Prefer to say too little than too much. If your partner has bid or played the hand like an idiot, say "bad luck" and leave it at that. Do not harp on past errors.

Use only the proper language of bridge. Use either "No bid" or "Pass" and stick to it. Do not switch back and forth between "Pass" and "No bid." Do not say "Content," "Okay," or "By me." Do not say "I'll double one heart." Just say "Double." Do not say "Spade" when you mean "One Spade."

Do not vary the intonation in your bidding (softly on weak hands, loudly on good ones). Never put a question mark at the end of your bid to make sure your partner understands that your 4NT is Blackwood or that your double is for takeout. That is quite atrocious. You are to convey messages to your partner by what you bid, not by the way you bid it. Frowns, scowls, raised eyebrows, and so on, are out. When written bidding is used, all bids should be with same strength of pen or pencil and all in the same size, not small writing with poor hands or large with strong hands. Avoid the tongue-in-cheek remark made by the legendary Groucho Marx: "Don't bother to signal. If you like my leads, just smile. I'll understand."

If your partner has a liberal sense of humor, you may be able to make clever remarks such as: "When did you learn? I know this afternoon, but what time?" or in reply to "How should I have played that hand?" "Under an assumed name," or in reply to "Did I do all right?" "Well, you didn't knock the coffee over," but in general, bridge players are a proud lot with sensitive egos. Make politeness and courtesy your trademark at the bridge table, as in other areas of life.

Long pauses before bidding are also to be avoided. For example, the pause followed by "Pass" tells everyone that you have 11–12 points, not quite good enough to open. Make all your bids at the same pace if you can. Sometimes you will have a serious problem, which takes some time to resolve. When this happens the obligation falls on your partner, who must never take advantage of the information received from the hesitation. As a defender, always play your cards at the same speed if possible. Fumbling or hesitating *with the intention of deceiving* is cheating. You must not try to mislead opponents by your manner.

In tournament bridge, if unsure about the correct procedure, always call the Tournament Director. Do not let other players tell you what the correct laws are. They are wrong more often than not. Nobody familiar with the tournament scene should mind the Director being called. It is not considered a slight, an insult, or a rebuff to the opposition.

Above all, bridge is primarily a game and is meant to be enjoyed as a game. Make sure it is also enjoyable for the other players at your table.

Appendix 8:
Tournament Bridge

Bridge is played internationally. In each odd-numbered year the Bermuda Bowl (World Open Teams), the Venice Cup (World Women's Teams), and the D'Orsi Bowl (World Seniors' Teams) are held and teams representing different geographical zones compete. When the World Bridge Teams are held in the Olympic years every country is entitled to compete. In the other even-numbered years there are the World Pairs Championships (open pairs, women's pairs, mixed pairs) as well as the World Teams Championships. These are open to virtually all players. World Junior Championships (under-26) are also played regularly.

Each country conducts national championships and many tournaments of lower status. There are also tournaments to select the players who will represent their country, their state or their club. The main kinds of competitive bridge are pairs events and teams events.

In general, pairs events are more common than any other type of event. The advantage of tournament bridge is that the element of having good cards or bad cards is reduced to a minimum, since all players play exactly the same deals. Another advantage is that you can compete against the top players merely by playing in the same tournament. In few other sports could a novice play against a world champion in a tournament. Tournament bridge also improves your game, since you can go over the hand records afterwards.

There are differences in technicalities and strategy between tournament bridge and social (or rubber) bridge. If the hands are pre-dealt, a common occurrence in the larger clubs, you must not shuffle and deal the cards. Otherwise, you shuffle and deal the cards at the first table, but not thereafter.

The cards come to you in a tray, called a "board" and you must put the cards back in the correct slot after the board has been played. The board is marked N, E, S, and W, and must be placed properly on the table; the board also states which side is vulnerable and who is the dealer. During the play, the cards are not thrown into the middle of the table. The players keep the cards in front of them, turning them face down after the trick is over. You may examine the trick just played only while your card remains face up. Tricks won are placed vertically, tricks lost are placed horizontally. After the hand is over, you can see at a glance how many tricks have been won and how many lost.

Each board in tournament bridge is scored independently. In rubber bridge, if you make a part score you have an advantage for the next deal, but in tournament bridge you do not carry forward any scores. You enter the score for the hand played, and on the next board both sides start from zero again.

As each deal is totally unrelated to what happened on the previous deal, there are significant scoring differences in tournament bridge:

(1) Honors do not count.

(2) For bidding and making a part score, add 50 to the trick total.

(3) For bidding and making a game not vulnerable, add 300 to the trick total.

(4) For bidding and making a game vulnerable, add 500 to the trick total.

The result you obtain on the board is entered on the "traveling score sheet" at the back of the board. You may not look at the sheet until the deal is over, since it contains the scores achieved by other pairs on that board and possibly a record of the deal. Your score on each board is compared with the scores of every other pair that played it. If you are North-South, your real opponents are all the other North-

South pairs, not the particular East-West pair you play each time. On each board, a certain number of match-points is awarded (usually one less than the number of pairs who play the board). If fifteen pairs play a board, the best score receives 14 match-points, a "top," the next best score receives 13, and so on down to the worst score which receives 0, a "bottom." An average score would receive 7 match-points. Scoring is done for the N-S pairs and also for the E-W pairs. Each pair's points over all the boards are totalled and the pair with the highest number of match-points wins.

Tactics in pairs events differ from those in rubber bridge. Careful play and defense are vital. Every overtrick and every undertrick can make the difference between a good score and a bad score. In rubber bridge, declarer's aim is almost always to make the contract and the defenders' aim is to defeat it. At pairs, the aim is to obtain the best possible score, which may mean that, as declarer, making the contract is a secondary consideration while, as a defender, the possibility of giving away an overtrick in trying to defeat the contract may be unwarranted.

Being extremely competitive in the bidding is essential. Almost always force the opposition to the three-level on part-score deals. Be quick to re-open the bidding if they stop at a very low level in a suit. In pairs events, re-opening the bidding occurs far more often than at rubber bridge.

Minor suit game contracts should be avoided. Prefer 3NT to 5♣ or 5♦, even if 3NT is riskier. Making one overtrick in 3NT scores more than a minor suit game. It is not necessary to bid borderline games or close slams. The reward for success in pairs events does not justify bidding 24 point games or 31 point slams. You should be in game or in slam if it has a 50 percent or better chance. If less, you will score better by staying out of it.

What counts at duplicate pairs is how often a certain strategy will work for you, not the size of the result. If a certain action scores 50 extra points eight times out of ten, but loses 500 twice, it is sensible at duplicate but ridiculous at rubber bridge. Penalty doubles are far more frequent at pairs since players are anxious to improve their score. The rule about a two-trick safety margin is frequently disregarded since one down, doubled, vulnerable, may be a top-score while one down, undoubled, vulnerable, may be below average.

Safety plays, which sacrifice a trick to ensure the contract, almost never apply in pairs, unless the contract reached is an unbelievably good one.

In the tournament world you will encounter a remarkable number and variety of systems and conventions. Gradually you will come to recognise them. The more important ones have been listed in Appendix 10. A most important point to remember is that a bidding system is not some secret code. You and your partner are not allowed to have any secret understanding about the meaning of your bids. That is *cheating.* The opponents are entitled to know as much about what the bidding means as you or your partner. If asked what you understand by a certain bid of your partner's, you must answer truthfully. Of course, your partner's bid may be meaningless and if you cannot understand it, all you can do is to be honest and tell the opposition that you do not know what your partner's bid means.

Similarly, if you do not understand the opposition's bidding, you are entitled to ask. When it is your turn to bid, but before you make your bid, you ask the partner of the bidder, "What do you understand by that bid?" You may ask during the auction or after the auction has ended, when it is your turn to play. Unless it affects your making a bid, prefer to wait until the auction is over. After all, the opposition might not understand their bidding either and when you ask, they may well realize their mistake.

If an irregularity occurs at the table, do not be dismayed if the Director is called. That is a normal part of the game and it is the Director's job to keep the tournament running smoothly and to sort out any irregularities.

Appendix 9:

How to Improve Your Game

(1) Play rubber bridge, for as high stakes as you can afford, with players who are better than you. This will cost you money, but the experience is invaluable and you will learn why they are better than you. You will scarcely improve (although you will undoubtedly enjoy your game) if you are better than the players with whom you are playing.

(2) Kibitz (watch) the best players in action either at tournaments or on the internet. Bridge Base Online is an excellent website, where you can often watch major tournaments with expert commentary. It costs nothing to watch experts play and few experts object to being watched. On the contrary it boosts their ego, and they may even explain why they made a certain bid or a certain play. To obtain the most benefit from kibitzing, watch one player exclusively. Try to decide what you would bid and play with the same cards. Then you can compare your solution with what the expert does in practice. If there is a startling discrepancy, you might ask for guidance. Most experts are happy to explain to those seeking to learn.

(3) Read bridge books. There are excellent books on bidding and on the play of the cards. Unfortunately there are a few that are mediocre. Ask an expert or a good bridge teacher for advice about what books you should be reading. At the early stages, books on card play are the better investment.

Controversy exists about whether bridge players are born or are made. It used to be the case that the natural player had a considerable edge over those who found bridge hard work. However, even the natural players now have to do a fair amount of bookwork to keep up with technical advances. Flair is certainly helpful, but expert technique is a skill that can be learned.

(4) Play tournament bridge as often as you can. Play with a partner who is better than you (if possible). Take particular notice of what happens when you come up against expert pairs. Pay attention to the bids they make, the leads they choose, and how they play as declarer or in defense.

(5) Join a bridge teaching website, such as www.ronklingerbridge. com, that is dedicated to helping all players to improve their standard. Whether you are a novice or an advanced player, there are daily problems and heaps of quizzes on bidding, declarer play, and defense to help you.

What is fascinating about bridge is that it can be enjoyed at all levels, but you will find that the better you play the more you enjoy it.

Appendix 10:

Popular Conventions and Systems

The following brief descriptions outline some of the popular conventions and systems that you may come across, particularly in tournament bridge. Before you adopt any of them, you should already be playing a sound game and, of course, you must discuss them fully with your partner first.

(1) Stayman 2♣ over a 1NT opening: This artificial inquiry asks whether the opener holds a 4-card major (see page 127). It is highly recommended and is used almost universally by tournament players.

(2) Stayman 3♣ over a 2NT opening: This is also highly recommended. (see page 128). It is superior to the Baron 3♣ convention (which after a 2NT opening asks the opener to bid 4-card suits up-the-line) since Stayman allows the strong hand to remain declarer more frequently and copes easily with 5-4 patterns as well as finding 4-4 fits.

(3) Blackwood 4NT asking for aces: This invaluable convention is almost universally played and is discussed in Chapter 8 (pages 81–87).

(4) Gerber 4♣ asking for aces: This convention asks for aces and kings like Blackwood 4NT except that the inquiry bid is 4♣. The replies are: 4♦ = 0 or 4; 4♥ = 1; 4♠ = 2; 4NT = 3. After the answer to 4♣, asking for kings is initiated by 5♣. Gerber 4♣ is rarely used by expert partnerships because it conflicts with Cue-Bidding.

(5) Cue-Bidding: This is a method of slam bidding in which partners tell each other which aces and kings are held as opposed to how many are held (which is the answer to 4NT Blackwood or 4♣ Gerber). It is a superior bidding method and is used widely among expert partnerships.

(6) Negative and competitive doubles: A better name for the negative double (pages 133–136) is responder's double, since it is simply a double for takeout by responder. Competitive doubles reflect the trend among top tournament players today to use virtually all doubles at the 1- or 2-level for takeout, almost regardless of the preceding auction. This sensible strategy should be adopted as soon as you have confidence and experience. In this style, it does not matter whether you are opener, responder, or a defender. If you double a suit bid at the 1- or 2-level, it is intended as a takeout double. The theory is that you will be dealt many more hands short in the enemy suit than those suitable for a penalty double at such a low level. If you have a hand suitable for penalties, pass and await your partner's re-opening takeout double, which you will pass.

(7) Weak No-Trumps: Not everyone uses the same point range for the 1NT opening. The most common range for the weak 1NT is 12–14, but occasionally the 13–15 range is used, as in the Precision system.

(8) Strong No-Trumps: The modern range for the strong no-trump is 15–17 points, but 16–18 or 15–18 point ranges are also popular.

(9) Weak Twos: This refers to 2♥, 2♠, and occasionally 2♦ openings on weak hands of 6–10 HCP with a strong 6-card suit. They are popular in tournament bridge, as they arise far more often than strong twos. They are both pre-emptive and constructive. Avoid a weak two with a void or two singletons in the hand or with a 4-card major. Pairs using weak twos may open super-strong hands with an artificial 2♣ (see page 76).

(10) Benjamin Twos: In this treatment for two-openings 2♥ and 2♠ are weak twos, 2♦ is a force to game (about 23 HCP or better), and 2♣ is a strong bid, but not forcing to game. 2♦ and 2♣ are both artificial. Your partner's negative reply is the next suit up. A positive reply to 2♣ is forcing to game and a positive reply to 2♦ strongly suggests slam. The 2♣ opening is generally based on a strong one-suiter, around 19–22 points (8½-9½ playing tricks), or a two-suiter around 21–22 points. This treatment is attractive because the partnership can bid both weak hands and strong hands more accurately than other systems of opening two-bids.

(11) Weak Jump-Overcalls: A treatment in which a single jump-overcall is played as a weak bid, around 6–10 HCP, and a 6-card or longer suit. The method is popular in tournament bridge but not at rubber (see page 97).

(12) Transfer Bids: A method in which a player bids the suit below the suit held. It is used normally only after a 1NT or 2NT opening and often enables the strong hand to become declarer in suit contracts. It also allows a partnership to bid many hands more accurately than in standard methods.

(13) Strong 1♣ Systems (such as Precision, Schenken, or Moscito): Systems in which the 1♣ opening bid shows any powerful hand, usually around 15–16 points or more. As a consequence, all other opening bids are limited in strength to less than the requirements for 1♣.

(14) Underleading honors: A system of opening leads where a player leads the second card from any sequence rather than the standard top of a sequence lead. From two honors doubleton, the top honor is led.

Appendix 11:

The Mechanics and Rules of Rubber Bridge

This appendix will clear up any queries you might have about the rules or procedure when playing bridge.

Bridge is a game for four players, playing in two partnerships. It represents a head-to-head battle—your side against theirs. Partners sit opposite each other. Partnerships are chosen by agreement or by lot. The common method is for each player to choose a card from the pack fanned out face down, with the players selecting the two highest cards forming one partnership against the players selecting the two lowest cards.

THE BRIDGE PACK

A regular pack of 52 cards is used and there are no jokers and no cards of any exceptional rank or function (unlike 500 where jacks have a special role, or Canasta where the 2s are jokers).

There are four suits:

♠ SPADES — ♥ HEARTS — ♦ DIAMONDS — ♣ CLUBS

Each suit consists of 13 cards which in order of rank are: Ace, King, Queen, Jack, 10, 9, 8, 7, 6, 5, 4, 3, 2. An ace beats a king, a king beats a queen, a queen beats a jack, a jack beats a ten, and so on. The top five cards in each suit (A, K, Q, J, and 10) are known as the honor cards or honors.

The suits also have a ranking order: CLUBS (♣) is the lowest suit, then come DIAMONDS (♦) and HEARTS (♥) to the highest-ranking suit, SPADES (♠). NO-TRUMPS ranks higher than any suit. The order of the suits—C, D, H, S—is no accident. They are in alphabetical order.

When selecting partnerships, if two cards of the same rank are chosen (e.g., two eights) and the tie needs to be broken, it is decided by suit order (e.g., the ♦8 would outrank the ♣8).

DEALING

The player who drew the highest card is the dealer on the first hand and has the right to choose seats and the pack of cards with which to deal. The next dealer will be the person on the left of the previous dealer and so on in clockwise rotation.

The cards are shuffled by the person on the dealer's left. The dealer passes the pack across the table to the person on the dealer's right to be cut. The dealer then deals the cards, one at a time, face down, in clockwise direction, starting with the player on the left, until all 52 cards are dealt, 13 each.

It is usual to leave your cards face down until the dealer has finished dealing. A misdeal may be corrected if the players have not seen their cards. While the dealer is dealing, the partner of the dealer shuffles the other pack for the next deal. Two packs are used to speed up game. The shuffler places the shuffled pack on the right, ready for the next dealer.

THE START OF PLAY

After picking up your cards, sort them into suits. Separating the red and the black suits makes it easy to see where one suit ends and the next begins.

The bidding starts with the dealer. After the bidding is over, the side that has bid higher wins the right to play the hand. One member of this side, called the declarer, plays the hand while the opponents defend the hand. The person on the left of declarer makes the opening lead. The partner of the declarer now puts all thirteen cards face up on the table and arranged in suits. The faced cards are called "the dummy." The dummy player takes no part in the play. Declarer plays both hands. Each player can see 26 cards, the 13 in hand plus the 13 in dummy.

Declarer plays a card from dummy, then the third player plays a card and so does declarer. The four cards now face up on the table are a "trick." A trick always consists of four cards played in clockwise sequence, one from each hand.

Each deal in bridge is a battle over thirteen tricks, declarer trying to win at least as many as nominated in the bidding, while the defenders try to win enough tricks to defeat declarer. The player who wins the trick gathers the four cards together, puts them face down neatly, and then leads to the next trick, and so on until all thirteen tricks have been played. (In tournament bridge, called "duplicate," the cards are not gathered together. The players keep their own cards in front of them.)

Following Suit

The player who plays the highest-ranking card of the suit led wins the trick. If two or more cards of the same rank are played to one trick, who wins then? The basic rule of play is: *You must follow suit*, i.e., you must play a card of the same suit as the suit led.

If a heart is led, you must play a heart if you have one and the trick is won by the highest heart played. If the two of hearts is led, and the other cards on the trick are the ten of hearts, the queen of spades, and the ace of clubs, the trick is won by the ten of hearts. If unable to follow suit, you may play any other card at all, but remember it is the highest card of the first led suit which wins. If the king of spades is led, it does you no good to play the ace of clubs. Only the ace of spades beats the king of spades.

Trumps

There is one exception. Where a suit has been nominated in the bidding as the *trump* suit, then any card in the trump suit is higher than any card in one of the other suits. If hearts are trumps, the two of hearts would beat the ace of clubs when clubs are led. But, first and foremost, you must follow suit. Only if you are out of a suit can you beat a high card of another suit with a trump. If you are unable to follow suit, you are allowed to trump, *but it is not obligatory.* You may choose to discard. For example, if your partner has won the trick, it may be foolish to trump your partner's winner.

A trick that does not contain a trump is won by the highest card in the suit led. A trick that contains a trump is won by the highest trump on the trick. If you fail to follow suit when able to do so, you have revoked (or "reneged"). The penalty for a revoke is to transfer one or two tricks to the other side—one trick if you do not win the revoking trick, two tricks if you do win the revoking trick.

THE BIDDING

The play is preceded by the bidding, also called "the auction." Just as in an auction an item goes to the highest bidder, so in the bridge auction each side tries to outbid the other for the right to be declarer and play the hand.

The dealer makes the first bid, then the player on the dealer's left and so on in clockwise rotation. Each player may decline to bid (say "Pass" or "No bid") or make a bid. A player who has previously passed may still make a bid later in the auction. A bid consists of a number (1, 2, 3, 4, 5, 6, or 7) followed by a suit or no-trumps, e.g., two spades, three hearts, four no-trumps, seven diamonds. "No-trumps" means that there is to be no trump suit on the deal.

Whenever a bid is made, the bidder is stating the number of tricks above six intended to be won in the play. The minimum number of tricks that you may contract for is seven. A bid of 1 Club contracts to make seven tricks with clubs as trumps.

The number in the bid is the number of tricks to be won *over and above six tricks.* Six tricks is not even halfway and you have to bid for more than half the tricks. The final bid is the "contract."

If all players pass without a bid on the first round there is no play, there is no score, the cards are thrown in, and the next dealer deals a new hand. When a bid is made on the first round, the auction has started and will be won by the side that bids highest. The auction continues, with each player making a bid or passing, and concludes as soon as a bid is followed by three passes. The side that bids higher sets the trump suit (or no-trumps) and the number of tricks to be won is set by the final bid. The member of the side who first bid the trump suit (or no-trumps) is the declarer.

After a bid, any player in turn may make a *higher* bid. A bid is higher than a previous bid if it is a larger number than the previous bid or the same number, but in a higher ranking denomination. The order of ranking is:

NO-TRUMPS SPADES HEARTS DIAMONDS CLUBS

A bid of 1 Heart is higher than a bid of l Club. If you want to bid clubs and the previous bid was 2 Spades, you would have to bid 3 Clubs (or 4 Clubs or 5 Clubs or higher). 2 Clubs would not be higher than 2 Spades.

GAMES

A rubber of bridge is over when one side wins two games. A game is won by scoring 100 or more points below the line when declarer. It is vital to understand how bridge is scored, for this affects the bidding and the play. You aim to score more points than the opposition. You may score points:

(1) by bidding and making a contract as declarer

(2) by defeating the opponents' contract

(3) by earning bonus points.

Some points are written above the line and some below the line on the scoresheet. When adding up the totals, all points count equally, but points below the line are especially valuable, since only these points count towards game. *Only the declarer side can score points for game.* That is the incentive for bidding higher than the opponents. *You score points below the line by bidding and making a contract,* according to this table:

NO-TRUMPS (NT)	40 points for the first trick (over six): 1NT = 40 30 for each subsequent trick: 2NT = 70, 3NT = 100 . . .
♠ SPADES	30 points for each trick (over six)—*major suit.*
♥ HEARTS	30 points for each trick (over six)—*major suit.*
♦ DIAMONDS	20 points for each trick (over six)—*minor suit.*
♣ CLUBS	20 points for each trick (over six)—*minor suit.*

Since game is 100 points or more, it takes 5 Clubs or 5 Diamonds to make game in a minor, while a bid of 4 Hearts or 4 Spades scores game in the major. In no-trumps, a bid of 3NT will score a game.

The declaring side gets credit not for the tricks won, but only for the tricks bid and then won. So if 4♥ is bid and declarer makes nine tricks, declarer does not get credit for nine tricks, but suffers a penalty for failing to make the contract by one trick. Thus accuracy in bidding distinguishes contract bridge from auction bridge (where you are given credit for what you make, even if you did not bid it) and becomes the single most important element in winning strategy. If declarer makes more tricks than the contract, the extra tricks ("overtricks") are not lost, but are scored as bonuses above the line.

Only points scored by winning the actual number of tricks of the contract are written below the line and only points below the line count towards winning games and the rubber.

A score below the line of less than 100 is a "partscore." Two or more partscores can be combined to score the 100 points for game. Points over 100 cannot be carried forward to the next game. After a game, both sides start the next game from zero. So, if you have a partscore, but the enemy score a game before you have been able to convert your partscore into a game, you start from zero for the next game. They have "underlined" you.

Doubles and Redoubles

Any player may double a bid made by an opponent by saying "Double." If there is no further bidding, the double increases the rewards for success and the penalties for failure. After a double, the other side may redouble (say "Redouble") increasing the rewards and penalties further.

A bid cancels any double or redouble, but there may be further doubles and redoubles of later bids. 1♠ making seven tricks scores 30, but 1♠ doubled and redoubled making seven tricks scores 120 below the line (and game!), plus 100 bonus points for making a redoubled contract ("for the insult").

Other Scoring

If in doubt, you can refer to the complete scoring table on pages 185–186. *You should know the trick value of each suit and no-trumps.* It is worth knowing some of the more common scores which go above the line, but the rest of the scoring can be learned gradually, as you play.

A side that has scored one game is said to be vulnerable and needs only one more game to complete the rubber. Penalties are more severe for failing to make a contract when vulnerable than when not vulnerable.

When one side fails to make its contract, the other side scores 50 points per undertrick if declarer is not vulnerable and 100 points per undertrick if declarer is vulnerable. These and all other bonus points go above the line. If the final contract is doubled or redoubled, the penalties are more severe (see the scoring table on pages 185–186). Note that penalties are the same whatever the contract. One down in 2♥ is the same as one down in 7NT.

You may score bonus points for each game (Game 1 +350, Game 2 +350, Game 3, if needed, +500) or enter these when the rubber is over (700 for 2 games to 0, 500 for 2 games to 1). For holding "honors" and also for overtricks in a doubled or redoubled contract, see the scoring table (pp. 185–186). The honor cards are the A, K, Q, J, and 10. Bonuses for honors are scored whether or not the contract is made. Honors may be held by declarer, dummy, or either defender. In order not to tell the opposition what cards you hold, honors are usually claimed after the hand has been played. Honors are not scored when playing duplicate.

A contract of six (twelve tricks) is a small slam. For a small slam bid and made, score above the line: 500 points if not vulnerable, 750 points if vulnerable.

A contract of seven (thirteen tricks) is a grand slam. Bid and make a grand slam and you score: 1,000 points if not vulnerable, 1,500 points if vulnerable. After deducting the losers' total from the winners' total, the net balance is rounded off to the nearest 100 (50 at the end of a score goes down). The score for the rubber is entered next to each player's name on a tally card and the next rubber is then started, either with the same partnerships or by drawing again for new partners. Bridge may be played with or without stakes. The amount of the stakes will be by agreement among the players. The stakes are usually stipulated at so much per hundred points, e.g., ten cents a hundred, one dollar a hundred.

Glossary and Index

TERM	EXPLANATION	PAGE
Balanced	A hand pattern of 4-3-3-3, 4-4-3-2, or 5-3-3-2	18
Bare	No further cards in a suit	23
Baron Convention	A 3♣ reply to a 2NT opening to ask for suits up-the-line	149
Benjamin Twos	A system of weak and strong two-openings	151
Big Club	Any system in which a 1♣ opening shows a strong hand	151
Blackwood	A conventional bid of 4NT asking for aces	82
Blocking	High cards preventing your cashing cards in the other hand	32
Cash	To play a winning card	31
Cheapest first	The way to bid 4-card suits as responder or rebid as opener	40
Competitive double	A low-level takeout double	150
Convention	Any artificial bid	149
Cue-Bidding	A method of showing specific aces, kings, and shortages	150
Doubleton	A suit consisting of exactly two cards	17–18
Drawing trumps	Playing trump cards to eliminate the opponents' trumps	52–53, 64–65
Duplicate	Tournament bridge	155

Term	Explanation	Page
8-ever, 9-never	A guide when to finesse for a missing queen	138
Exit	To lead a card without expectation of winning the trick	65, 74, 114
Finesse	An attempt to win a trick with a card lower than theirs	64–65, 74–75
5-3-1 count	Points counted for voids, singletons, and doubletons	45
Forcing bid	A bid that requires your partner to bid again	66–67, 98
4-3-2-1 count	Points counted for aces, kings, queens, and jacks	17
Gambling raise	A raise from the 1-level to the 4-level or 5-level	44
Game-force	A bid that requires the bidding to continue to game	98, 107
2♣ game-force	An artificial opening bid normally leading to game or slam	76
2♦ game-force	Part of Benjamin Twos, artificial and usually game forcing	151
Gerber	A convention where 4♣ asks how many aces your partner holds	149
HCP	High card points	17
High-from-shortage	Playing high cards first from the shorter holding	31, 36–37
Honor card	An ace, king, queen, jack, or ten	160
Interior sequence	Honor card, gap, then a sequence headed by an honor card	31
Invitational bid	A bid asking your partner to bid on if better than minimum	117
Jump-raise	A raise that skips one or more levels of bidding	44

TERM	EXPLANATION	PAGE
Jump-shift	A bid in a new suit that skips one level of bidding	46, 55, 56
Length points	Points counted for each card in a suit beyond four	27, 28
Limited bid	A bid that has a narrow point range, e.g., 15–17, 12–14	39
Marked finesse	A finesse that you know will succeed	64–65
MUD	Middle Up Down—a system of leads from rag cards	131
Negative double	A double for takeout by responder	133–136, 150
Not vulnerable	Not having won a game in the current rubber	123
One-suiter	A hand containing only one suit of 4 or more cards	19
Opening bid	The first bid in the auction (Pass is not a bid)	95
Opening lead	The first card played on the first trick	129, 151
Overcall	A bid after an opponent has opened the bidding	95–98
Over-ruff	To ruff higher than the trump used by an opponent to ruff	65, 75
Overtaking	Playing a higher card on a high card of your own	32, 37
Pattern	The number of cards held in each suit	17
Penalty double	A double asking your partner to pass and defend	115–117
Pre-emptive bid	Intended to shut the opponents out of the bidding	88–90
Renege	To revoke	156

TERM	EXPLANATION	PAGE
Rescue	To remove a bid made by your partner because you fear your partner's contract will fail	116
Revoke	Failure to follow suit when able to do so	156
Ruff	To trump	117
Rubber	The unit of play at rubber bridge	121
Sacrifice	To bid above the opponents' bid for a smaller loss	21
Semi-balanced	The shape for a 5-4-2-2, 6-3-2-2, or 7-2-2-2 pattern	18
Shape	Hand type according to the number of short suits held	17–18
Shortage points	Points counted for a void, singleton, or doubleton	39, 45
Shutout bid	Designed to keep the opposition out of the bidding	44
Signoff bid	A bid intended to end the auction	173, 183
Singleton	A holding of one card in a suit	17–18
Sluff or slough	Jargon for "discard" (e.g. a ruff-and-sluff)	- - -
Stayman Convention	A response of 2♣ to 1NT to ask for a major suit	127
Stiff	Jargon for "singleton"	23
Stopper	A holding of the ace, K-x, Q-x-x, J-x-x-x, or better	95, 98
Takeout double	A double asking your partner to bid and remove the double	105–108
Tenace	Two high cards with a gap between them and an opponent holding the card(s) in-between	65, 87
Three-suiter	A hand with a 4-4-4-1 or 5-4-4-0 pattern	19
Tight	Jargon for "no more cards in the suit"	23

TERM	EXPLANATION	PAGE
Top of sequence	System of leads from a run of three or more honors	31–32, 52–53
Transfer bid	Conventional bid of the suit below your real suit	151
Two-suiter	A hand containing two suits of four or more cards	19
Unbalanced	Shape of any hand pattern with a void or a singleton	18
Underleading	System of leading 2nd highest card from a sequence	151
Unlimited bid	Bid with a very wide range of points, e.g. 12–21, 6–18	39
Up-the-line	The order in which two or three 4-card suits are bid	40
Void	Holding no cards in a suit	18
Vulnerable	Having won one game	159
Weak freak	Characteristics of a shut-out jump raise	44
Weak takeout	Removal of 1NT into 2-of-a-suit as a signoff	107
Weak two	Opening bid of 2-in-a-suit as a weak bid	150

Answers to Exercises and Bidding Practice

Page   Answers

20 **Exercise 1:** 1. Unbalanced 2. Unbalanced 3. Semi-balanced 4. Balanced 5. Balanced 6. Balanced 7. Unbalanced 8. Unbalanced

Exercise 2:

	A	B	C	D
Hand 1	13	Semi-balanced	5-4-2-2	2-suiter
Hand 2	14	Balanced	4-4-3-2	2-suiter
Hand 3	14	Balanced	4-3-3-3	1-suiter
Hand 4	13	Unbalanced	5-5-2-1	2-suiter
Hand 5	11	Semi-balanced	6-3-2-2	1-suiter
Hand 6	12	Unbalanced	6-5-2-0	2-suiter
Hand 7	14	Unbalanced	4-4-4-1	3-suiter
Hand 8	13	Unbalanced	6-4-3-0	2-suiter

30 1. One club 2. One heart 3. Pass 4. One heart 5. One spade. Higher ranking first with 5-5 patterns. 6. One spade 7. One heart 8. One diamond. Longer suit first even with a 5-card major as well. 9. Pass. With 12 HCP and a 4-3-3-3, pass in first or second seat. In third or fourth seat, you may open even with less if you have a strong suit. 10. One diamond 11. One club 12. One club. With 3-3 in the minors, open one club regardless of suit quality. (4-card suits: open one spade.) 13. One club 14. One club 15. One diamond. 4-4 in the minors: open one diamond. (Modern 4-suits: One club) 16. One diamond (Goren: One spade) 17. One diamond (Goren: One spade) 18. One club 19. One diamond

(Modern 4-suits: One club) 20. One diamond (Modern 4-suits: One club; Goren: One heart) 21. Pass 22. One spade. 11 HCP is enough if you have a 6-card suit or two 5-card suits. 23. One spade 24. One club 25. One diamond. With no 5-card suit, open the longer minor. (Goren: One spade; Modern 4-suits: One heart) 26. One club. Longer minor. (Goren: One spade. Modern 4-suits: One heart) 27. One diamond. 4-4 minors. (Modern 4-suits: Open one club) 28. One club. 3-3 minors. (Modern 4-suits: One heart)

35 **Exercise A:** 1. 1NT. You do not need a stopper in every suit to open 1NT. 2. 1NT. The 5-3-3-2 is a balanced shape. 3. 1NT. In the modern style, most top players prefer to open 1NT even with a 5-3-3-2 and a 5-card major if the point count is right. 4. One diamond. When beyond 1NT and below 2NT, start with a suit opening. You plan to rebid with a jump in no-trumps.

Exercise B: 1. 3NT. 2. Pass. With 15-17 opposite, there cannot be 26 points together. 3. 2NT. 4. 3NT. The 5-3-3-2 is a balanced shape.

Partnership Bidding Practice: 1. Pass: 1NT, Pass 2. 1NT: 2NT, Pass 3. Pass: 1NT, 3NT. 3NT is a good spot, but 4 spades is almost hopeless. 4. 1NT: 2NT, Pass. Treat 16 points and a 4-3-3-3 pattern as a minimum. 5. Pass: 1NT, 2NT: 3NT. Opener with 17 should accept the 2NT invitation. 6. 1NT: Pass 7. 1NT: Pass. Seven points in a balanced hand is not enough to make a move towards game. 8. Pass: 1NT, 3NT.

42 **(a)** 1. One diamond. Longest suit first. 2. One heart. Up-the-line with 4-card suits. 3. One spade 4. One spade. Show a major rather than support a minor. 5. One heart. There is no suit quality requirement when bidding a 4-card suit. 6. One diamond. Longer suit first. 7. One heart. Even a 4-card major should be shown before showing 5-card or better support for a minor. 8. Pass. Too weak to reply even if you do not like the suit your partner opened.

(b) 1. One spade. Show even a weak major before supporting a minor. 2. One heart 3. One spade 4. One spade 5. One heart 6. One spade. Technically the major suit should be shown before raising the diamonds. However, five diamonds would be a sensible, practical bid. 7. One heart. Too weak for two clubs (showing 10 or more points). 8. Pass.

(c) 1. One spade. Too weak for two diamonds. 2. Two hearts. If the values allow, support a major rather than change suit. 3. One spade. 4. One spade 5. Two hearts 6. One spade. Very close between this and two diamonds. 7. Two hearts 8. Pass. Even with such good support, the hand is too weak to give a raise.

(d) 1. Two spades 2. Two spades 3. Two spades 4. Two spades 5. Two spades 6. Four spades. A practical shot. 7. One no-trump. Too weak for two clubs. 8. Pass

Exercise A: 1. One no-trump. With a 4-3-3-3 pattern, prefer 1NT to raising the clubs. 2. One diamond. Change suit rather than respond 1NT. 3. One heart. Major suit *openings* show five; responder's suits normally promise *four* or more. 4. One spade 5. One diamond. 4-card suits go up-the-line, even with the diamonds. 6. One heart 7. One spade. Show the major rather than raise a minor. 8. One diamond 9. One spade. Higher-ranking suit first when holding a 5-5 pattern. 10. One spade. Show the major before raising a minor. 11. One diamond. Up-the-line. 12. One heart. Show the major, up-the-line, before raising a minor. 13. One spade 14. Two clubs. Raise a minor rather than show the other minor. 15. Two clubs 16. One diamond. Longest suit first.

43   **Exercise B:** 1. One spade. Up-the-line means "cheapest suit first." One spade is cheaper than two clubs. 2. One spade. Any suit quality is acceptable for a 4-card suit. 3. One no-trump. Too weak for two clubs. 4. One spade. Too weak for two diamonds which shows 10 points or more. With insufficient points, you have to bid the shorter suit first. 5. Two hearts. 6. Two hearts 7. Two hearts.

Raise the major rather than show the other major. 8. One no-trump. Too weak for two clubs. The 1NT response may include a singleton or a void. 9. One spade 10. One no-trump 11. One no-trump 12. Two hearts. Three points for the singleton makes this quite strong enough to raise to the two-level.

51 9. 1 club: 1 diamond, 1 spade: 1NT, Pass 10. 1 club: 1 heart, 2NT: 3 hearts, 4 hearts: Pass 11. Pass: 1 club, 2 clubs: 3NT, Pass 12. 1 club: 1 diamond, 1 heart: 2 hearts, Pass 13. Pass: 1 club, 1 spade: 4 spades, Pass 14. 1 spade: 1NT, 3 hearts: 4 hearts, Pass 15. Pass: 1 heart, 2 hearts: 3 hearts, 4 hearts: Pass 16. 1 spade: 1NT, 3NT: Pass 17. Pass: 1 diamond, 1NT: Pass 18. 1 diamond: 1 heart, 1 spade: 2 diamonds, Pass 19. Pass: 1 club, 1 heart: 1 spade, 2 spades: Pass 20. 1 club: 1 heart, 1 spade: 2 spades, 4 spades: Pass

58 **A.** 1. 3NT 2. 1 diamond 3. 1 diamond. No spade stopper makes 3NT unattractive. 4. 1 heart. Prefer a major to a reply in no-trumps. 5. 1 diamond. 4-card suits up-the-line. 6. 1 heart 7. 1 diamond 8. 1 heart. No need to rush with a strong hand.
B. 1. 3 diamonds 2. 1 heart 3. 1 heart 4. 1 spade
C. 1. 3 hearts 2. 1 spade. Do not give a jump raise with only three trumps 3. 2 clubs. 4-card suits up-the-line. 4. 2 diamonds
D. 1. 2 diamonds 2. 2 hearts 3. 2 diamonds 4. 2 diamonds. Much too strong for 2 spades and also too strong for 3 spades. With such hands, change suit first and support later.
E. 1. 3 spades 2. 3 no-trumps 3. 4 hearts 4. 3 hearts

61 **A.** 1. 3 no-trumps 2. 3 hearts 3. 3 clubs 4. Pass
B. 1. 2 no-trumps. Shows a minimum balanced hand. 2. 3 no-trumps 3. 2 diamonds 4. 3 clubs
C. 1. 2 diamonds 2. 2 hearts. Not strong enough to bid 2 spades. A new suit rebid above 2 of the opened suit shows 16 points or more. 3. 2 hearts 4. 2 hearts 5. 2NT 6. 3NT 7. 2 spades 8. 2 diamonds

D. 1. 3 spades 2. 4 hearts 3. 3 no-trumps 4. 3 diamonds
E. 1. 2 hearts 2. 2 spades. Not strong enough for 3 clubs. A new suit beyond 2 of the suit opened = 16+ points. 3. 3 spades 4. 4 spades

62   21. 1 club: 1 diamond, 1 spade: 3NT, Pass 22. 1 club: 1 diamond, 1 spade: 3NT, 4 spades: 5 clubs, Pass 23. 1 club: 1 heart, 3 clubs: 3 diamonds, 3NT 24. 1 club: 1 heart, 2 clubs: 2 diamonds, 3 hearts: 4 hearts, Pass 25. 1 club: 1 diamond, 1 heart: 1 spade, 2 spades: 4 spades, Pass 26. 1 club: 1 diamond, 1 heart: 3 diamonds, 3NT: Pass 27. 1 diamond : 2 clubs, 2NT: Pass
28. 1 diamond: 1 heart, 2 clubs: 3 clubs, 3NT: Pass
29. 1 diamond: 2 clubs, 2 diamonds: 2 hearts, 3 hearts: 4 hearts, Pass
30. 1 diamond: 1 heart, 2 clubs: 3 hearts, 4 hearts : Pass
31. 1 diamond: 1 heart, 2 diamonds: 3NT, Pass
32. 1 diamond: 1 spade, 2 clubs: 2 hearts, 3 clubs: 3NT, Pass

63   33. 1 heart: 1 spade, 2 hearts: 3 clubs, 3 spades: 4 spades, Pass
34. 1 heart: 1 spade, 2 hearts: 3 clubs, 3NT: Pass
35. 1 heart: 2 clubs, 2 diamonds: 2NT, 3NT: Pass
36. 1 heart: 2 clubs, 2 spades: 3 clubs, 3NT: Pass
37. 1 heart: 1 spade, 2 spades: 4 spades, Pass
38. 1 heart: 2 diamonds, 3 diamonds: 3 hearts, 4 hearts: Pass
39. 1 spade: 2 diamonds, 2 hearts: 2 spades, 4 spades: Pass
40. 1 spade: 2 diamond, 2 hearts: 2NT, 3 hearts: 4 hearts, Pass
41. 1 spade: 2 diamonds, 2 hearts: 2NT, 3NT: Pass
42. 1 spade: 2 hearts, 3 diamonds: 3 hearts, 4 hearts: Pass
43. 1 spade: 2 hearts, 2 spades: Pass
44. 1 spade: 2 hearts, 3 hearts: 4 hearts, Pass

68   **A.** 1. 2 no-trumps 2. 1 heart 3. 2 spades 4. 3 clubs
B. 1. 3 hearts 2. 2 hearts 3. 2 no-trumps 4. 2 spades
5. 1 spade 6. 2 diamonds 7. 1 no-trump 8. 3 hearts
Partnership Bidding: 45. Pass: 1 heart, 3 hearts: 4 hearts, Pass

46. Pass: 1 club, 1 heart: 1 spade, 3 spades: 4 spades, Pass
47. Pass: 1 spade, 2 diamonds: Pass 48. Pass: 1 club, 1 spade: Pass
49. Pass: 1 club, 3 clubs: 3NT, Pass 50. Pass: 1 spade, 2 clubs: Pass

72 **A.** 1. 2 hearts 2. 2 diamonds 3. 2 hearts 4. 1 spade. Not enough
for a 2-opening 5. 2 hearts 6. 2 clubs
B. 1. 2 no-trumps 2. 2 no-trumps 3. 3 no-trumps 4. 3 diamonds 5.
3 hearts 6. 3 hearts 7. 4 hearts. Weaker than 3 hearts 8. 2 spades
C. 1. 3 hearts 2. 4 spades 3. 3 spades 4. 3 no-trumps 5. 6 hearts.
This shows you have twelve tricks in your own hand and asks your
partner to choose between hearts and spades. Your partner may
revert to 6 spades and should bid seven if holding the spade king.
6. 3 clubs

73 **D.** 1. 3 no-trumps 2. 4 spades. Weaker than 3 spades. 3. 3 spades
4. 4 diamonds 5. 4 hearts 6. 4 spades 7. 3 no-trumps 8. 5 hearts
E. 1. 6 hearts 2. Pass 3. 7 diamonds 4. 7 hearts
51. 2 diamonds: 2NT, 3 spades: 3NT, Pass
52. Pass: 2 clubs, 2 diamonds: 2 spades, 3NT: 4 spades, Pass
53. 2 spades: 2NT, 3 spades: 4 spades, Pass
54. 2 diamonds: 2NT, 3 diamonds: 3 spades, 3NT: Pass
55. Pass: 2 spades, 2NT: 3 hearts, 4 hearts: Pass
56. Pass: 2NT, 3NT: Pass

84 **A.** 1. Slam zone. Bid 3 spades for now. Even if your partner cannot
support spades, you are still strong enough for 6NT. 2. Slam zone.
Bid 3 diamonds for now. 3. Game zone. Bid 3NT. 14 points plus
15-17 does not add up to 33 points. 4. Game zone. Pass. 4 hearts
is a weak, shut-out raise. 5. Game zone. Bid 4 hearts. 6. Slam
zone. Your partner's jump shows 6 hearts and 16 points or more.
Bid 4NT, asking for aces.
B. 1. 5 spades, showing three aces 2. 5 clubs, showing none or four
aces 3. 5 hearts. Two aces are missing. 4. 5 diamonds, showing one

ace 5. Pass. Five hearts was a sign-off. The 4NT asker is in charge of how high to bid. Five hearts implies two aces are missing. 6. 6 hearts, showing two kings

85 **C. a.** 6 spades. With one ace missing, bid the small slam. Do not stop in 5 spades. **b.** 6 spades. One king is missing and you cannot tell which one it is. **c.** 7NT. Your partner has shown spade support, three aces and two kings. That should give you thirteen tricks easily.

D. a. Pass. The 4NT bidder is in control of the slam decisions. Your partner needs no support from you. Your partner's diamonds will be self-sufficient. **b.** 6 spades. Here your partner has bid two suits, spades first and diamonds later. Your partner is asking you to choose the trump suit. You clearly prefer the spades. **c.** 6 spades. This is the rare exception when you may overrule your partner's intended sign-off. You have undisclosed support and an outside void.

E. a. 5 no-trumps. Your partner is attempting to sign off in no-trumps. Your partner cannot bid 5NT as this asks for kings. Bidding an unbid suit at the 5-level asks your partner to bid 5NT which can then be passed. Apparently two aces are missing **b.** Pass. The raise to five in a major asks your partner to bid six with strong trumps. Your trumps are no better than expected for a 1 spade opening. **c.** 6 hearts. You have strong hearts and that is what your partner is asking of you.

Partnership Bidding: 57. 2 spades: 3 clubs, 3 hearts: 4 no-trumps, 5 spades: 6 no-trumps, Pass 58. 1 no-trump: 6 no-trumps, Pass 59. Pass: 2 hearts, 3 hearts: 4 no-trumps, 5 diamonds: 5 no-trumps, 6 hearts : 7NT. On finding heart support plus an ace and two kings with West, East can count thirteen tricks.

60. 1 spade: 2 clubs, 2 hearts: 4 hearts, 4 no-trumps: 5 hearts, 5 no-trumps: 6 diamonds, 6 hearts: Pass

61. 2 no-trumps: 7 no-trumps. With no-trump hands, it is just a matter of adding the points together.

62. 2 hearts: 2 no-trumps, 3 diamonds: 3 hearts, 4 no-trumps: 5 clubs, 5 no-trumps: 6 hearts, 7 no-trumps: Pass. Opposite two kings, West can count thirteen tricks once the hearts were supported.

91 **A.** 1. Eight 2. Seven 3. Six 4. Seven and a half 5. Six and a half 6. Six 7. Six 8. Six 9. Four 10. Five 11. Six 12. Seven 13. Six 14. Five 15. Five 16. Six 17. Four 18. Six
B. (i) 1. 4 spades 2. 4 hearts 3. 1 club. Too strong for a pre-empt. 4. 5 diamonds 5. 4 spades. Expectancy is eight playing tricks. 6. 3 clubs. A pre-empt with only a 6-card suit is rare but if the suit is strong and you have the right number of playing tricks, it is all right. 7. Pass 8. Pass. Do not pre-empt with a 4-card major on the side. 9. Pass. The spades are too weak. Only five playing tricks potential. 10. Pass. If you must bid, open 1 spade. 11. One heart. Too strong for a pre-empt. 12. 4 hearts. The typical pre-empt has a long strong suit and little else. 13. Pass. Only five playing tricks potential. 14. 2 spades. Do not pre-empt when you have a powerful hand. 15. 4 spades. It is all right to have a 4+ minor suit on the side.
(ii) 1. 3 spades. Seven playing tricks. When vulnerable, add two to your playing trick potential. 2. 3 hearts 3. 1 club 4. 5 diamonds 5. 4 spades 6. Pass 7. Pass 8. Pass 9. Pass 10. Pass 11. 1 heart 12. 3 hearts 13. Pass 14. 2 spades 15. 4 spades. Optimistic, perhaps, but there are six playing tricks in spades and there could be two in clubs.

92 **C.** (i) 1. Pass 2. Pass 3. Pass. Do not "rescue" your partner on a misfit with a weak hand. 4. 3 spades. Your Partner should support with a doubleton or better. 5. Pass. You need more than three winners to raise a non-vulnerable pre-empt. 6. 4 hearts. Three winners plus potential for a fourth trick via a spade ruff. 7. 3 no-trumps. With a double stopper in every suit outside your partner's, this is a sound risk with a balanced hand. 8. 4 hearts. With nine hearts between you, spades is unlikely to be a better trump fit. 9. 4 hearts 10. Pass

11. 4 no-trumps. If your partner has the ace of hearts, you should bid 7NT. 12. 4 no-trumps. If your partner has an ace, bid 6 hearts.
(ii) 1. Pass 2. Pass 3. Pass 4. 3 spades 5. 4 hearts. To raise a vulnerable pre-empt, more than two winners is enough. 6. 4 hearts 7. 3 no-trumps 8. 4 hearts 9. 4 hearts 10. Pass 11. 4 no-trumps 12. 4 no-trumps

Partnership Bidding: 63. 3 spades: 4 spades, Pass

64. 3 diamonds: 3NT, Pass

65. 3 diamonds: 3 spades, 4 spades: Pass

66 . Pass: 3 hearts, Pass

67. 4 spades: 4NT, 5 diamonds : 6 spades, Pass

68. 3 diamonds: 3 hearts, 4 hearts: 4NT, 5 diamonds: 6 hearts, Pass. Change of suit is forcing after a pre-empt. Once East receives heart support, slam should be bid if West shows an ace.

99 **A.** 1. Pass 2. Bid 1NT. 3. Pass. You diamonds are much too weak for an overcall. 4. Pass. With length and strength in the enemy suit, the best strategy in most cases is to pass and defend.
B. 1. 1 spade 2. 1 spade 3. Pass 4. 1 diamond 5. Pass 6. 4 spades 7. 1 spade. With a 5-5 pattern, start with the higher-ranking suit. 8. 2 hearts. Strong jump overcall. 9. Pass. Suit too weak to overcall.
C. 1. 2 diamonds 2. Pass. Suit too weak to overcall. 3. 3 clubs. Strong jump-overcall. You hope your partner can bid 3NT. 4. 3 no-trumps. You figure to take nine tricks on a spade lead. 3NT is a good gamble. 5. 2 hearts 6. Pass 7. 5 diamonds. Pre-emptive. Worth the risk. 8. 2 diamonds 9. Pass. The clubs do not meet the Suit Quality Test for the two-level and the spade length is a drawback to an overcall.

100 **D.** 1. Pass 2. 1 spade 3. 4 spades. Bid up on the freak hands.
E. 1. Pass. If the opponents' bidding is genuine, your partner can have scarcely one point. 2. 4 hearts. A reasonable shot. 3. Pass. As with the first hand, your partner can have very little. Your hand is

good for defending, not so good for playing, with only 5-6 tricks potential.

F. 1. Pass 2. 4 hearts 3. 2 hearts 4. 3 hearts 5. 2 diamonds 6. 1 no-trump 7. 2 no-trumps 8. 1 spade 9. 3 no-trumps

101 **G.** 1. 3 spades 2. 4 spades 3. 2 no-trumps

102 **Partnership Bidding:** 69. (1 club) 1 heart: 1 no-trump, 2 hearts: Pass
70. (1 club): 1 no-trump: 4 hearts, Pass
71. (1 diamond): 2 hearts: 4 hearts, Pass
72. (1 diamond): 1 heart: 3 hearts, 4 hearts: Pass
73. (1 heart): 1 no-trump: 2 no-trumps, 3 no-trumps: Pass
74. (1 heart): 2 spades: 4 spades, Pass
75. (1 heart): 2 diamonds: 2 spades, 3 spades: 4 spades, Pass
76. (1 spade): 2 clubs: 2 no-trumps, 3 no-trumps: Pass
77. (1 spade): Pass: 3 hearts, 4 hearts: Pass
78. (1 spade): 2 clubs: 3 no-trumps, Pass

109 **A.** 1. Takeout 2. Takeout 3. Takeout 4. Penalties 5. Penalties. Double of a 1NT opening is for penalties. 6. Penalties. Double after a 1NT opening is for penalties.
B. 1. Double 2. Double 3. 1 diamond. Lack of support for hearts makes this unattractive for a double. 4. Double. If your partner bids diamonds, you can bid hearts. 5. Double. With only four losers, the hand is too powerful for even a strong jump-overcall. 6. 1 spade. Lack of heart support makes a double unappealing. 7. Double. 8. 1 no-trump. If the hand fits a 1NT overcall, prefer that bid. 9. Double. Double-and-no-trumps-later is stronger than 1NT at once.
C. 1. Pass 2. Pass. With 12–15 HCP, if your hand is not suitable for an overcall or a takeout double, pass. You are expected to open with 13 points but you need not take action with an unsuitable 13-

point hand after the opposition have opened. 3. Double. The right ingredients for a takeout double with minimum point count are shortage in the enemy suit and 3-4 cards in each of the other suits. 4. 1 spade. Prefer to show a strong 5-card or longer holding in the other major by bidding the major. 5. Double. With only four cards in the other major, double works better and is superior to bidding the diamonds. 6. Pass. The more you have in their suit, the better it is to defend. 7. 1 no-trump. If the conditions are right, prefer 1NT to a double. 8. Double. Too strong for 1NT. 9. Double. Too big for even a strong jump-overcall. (and only 5 spades)

110 **D.** 1. 1 spade 2. 1 spade. This hand makes Hand 1 look great. 3. 1 spade 4. 1 heart. Choose a major rather than a minor in response to a double even when the major is shorter or weaker. 5. 2 clubs 6. 1 heart. With no 4-card suit to bid (you would not want to bid their suit), choose your cheapest 3-card suit.
E. 1. 2 spades. Too strong for 1 spade. Worth 10 points once you count your singleton. 2. 2 hearts. Too big for 1 heart. Count your doubletons and you have 10 points. 3. 2 diamonds. Not 1 diamond. 4. 1 no-trump 5. 2 no-trumps 6. 4 spades. A sound approach when answering a takeout double is to imagine your partner has opened in your best suit. If your partner had opened 1 spade, you would not settle for less than game.

111 **F.** 1. Pass. You are no longer obliged to bid. 2. 2 hearts. However, you are not forced to pass. Over an intervening bid, you should bid with 6 points or more. Again, imagine your partner had opened 1 heart. You would not hesitate then to bid 2 hearts over a 1 spade overcall. 3. 3 hearts. If you are worth a jump, make the jump-reply over the intervention. Had South passed, you would have jumped to 2 hearts.
G. 1. Pass. 2. 2 hearts 3. 3 hearts. Your partner may have no points.

112 **Partnership Bidding:** 79. (1 heart): Double: 2 diamonds, Pass
  80. (1 heart): Double: 2 clubs, Pass
  81. (1 club): Double: 1 spade, 2 spades: Pass
  82. (1 club): Double: 1 heart, 3 hearts: Pass
  83. (1 diamond): Double: 1 spade, Pass
  84. (1 heart): Double: 1 no-trump, 2 no-trumps: 3 no-trumps, Pass
  85. (1 spade): Double: 2 no-trumps, 3 no-trumps: Pass
  86. (1 heart) : Double: 2 spades, Pass
  87. (1 club): Double: 4 spades, Pass
  88. (1 diamond): Double: 3 clubs, 3 hearts: 4 hearts, Pass

Play Hands for NORTH (* = dealer)

1*	2	3	4	5*	6
♠ A Q J 7	♠ Q 10 9 2	♠ 7 5 4 3	♠ J 9 2	♠ A Q 5 3	♠ K 10 9 7 4
♥ 9 4 3	♥ 3 2	♥ Q J 10 9	♥ A K 2	♥ 8 6 3	♥ 10
♦ Q 7 5	♦ J 6	♦ K Q 10	♦ K Q J	♦ 7 4 2	♦ 10 5 2
♣ 6 4 2	♣ 9 8 7 5 4	♣ 10 6	♣ 8 6 3 2	♣ 10 8 5	♣ 10 8 4 3

7	8	9*	10	11	12
♠ Q 9 8	♠ 8 7 4	♠ A K Q 9 8 3	♠ 10 6	♠ 5 3	♠ 5 4
♥ 7 6 5 4	♥ Q 9 6	♥ A 8 6	♥ 8 2	♥ 9 2	♥ 8 6
♦ A Q	♦ Q 8	♦ Q 3	♦ 9 8 4 3	♦ K Q 9 3	♦ A 10 9 3 2
♣ A K Q 6	♣ K J 9 4 2	♣ J 10	♣ K 10 6 4 2	♣ J 8 7 4 2	♣ 10 7 5 4

13*	14	15	16	17*	18
♠ 10 7 4	♠ - - -	♠ A 9 7 5	♠ - - -	♠ A Q J 3	♠ 10
♥ A K Q 10	♥ 10 8 5 4	♥ K Q 4 2	♥ 10 9 6 3 2	♥ A K	♥ J 10 9 5 3 2
♦ K	♦ A 7 5 3	♦ 8 5 2	♦ 9 7 5 4 2	♦ A J 4 2	♦ 9 8
♣ J 8 7 6 2	♣ 8 7 4 3 2	♣ K Q	♣ A K 8	♣ Q J 9	♣ A 8 7 2

19	20	21*	22	23	24
♠ A	♠ 8	♠ 9 6 5 2	♠ J 6	♠ A K Q J 2	♠ Q 10 9
♥ 8 6 5 3 2	♥ Q J 9 7 4	♥ J 10 9 4 3	♥ 9 7 5 3 2	♥ K Q J 4	♥ J 10 9 8
♦ 7 4 3 2	♦ Q 10 7 4 2	♦ 6 5 2	♦ A 2	♦ A Q J	♦ Q 10 9
♣ 7 5 3	♣ 9 2	♣ 10	♣ A Q J 5	♣ 2	♣ 9 6 5

25*	26	27	28	29*	30
♠ A K Q 9 7 6 5	♠ K Q 7 6	♠ J	♠ 10 6 4 3 2	♠ A K	♠ 6 5
♥ 2	♥ K 10 8 7 3	♥ A Q J	♥ - - -	♥ K 8 6 2	♥ 2
♦ 8	♦ J 9 8	♦ K 10 9	♦ K 9 3 2	♦ K Q 10 9 3	♦ J 7 6 4 3
♣ 9 8 7 3	♣ 2	♣ A 9 8 7 6 3	♣ 10 8 7 6	♣ 10 5	♣ J 7 5 4 2

31	32	33*	34	35	36
♠ 5 2	♠ A K	♠ J 10 8 7 4 3	♠ 8	♠ A K Q J	♠ K Q J 10 7
♥ A 9 3 2	♥ A 10 9 8 5 2	♥ 6	♥ K J 10 6 5 4	♥ K 7 5 3	♥ K 8 6 2
♦ 8 2	♦ K 3	♦ 10 9 5	♦ A 6	♦ K	♦ 9 4
♣ J 9 8 6 4	♣ K J 10	♣ J 5 3	♣ J 9 6 2	♣ Q 4 3 2	♣ A 10

Play Hands for EAST (* = dealer)

1	2*	3	4	5	6*
♠ 109432	♠ A J 3	♠ A K 10 2	♠ 10 8 7 5 3	♠ 10 9 8 2	♠ 8 5 3
♥ 5	♥ Q 5 4	♥ A 4	♥ Q 7 6	♥ Q 5 4	♥ A 4 3 2
♦ J 10 9 6	♦ A K 5 2	♦ 6 4 3	♦ 9 7 2	♦ K Q J 9	♦ A K Q J
♣ K Q 10	♣ 10 6 3	♣ 8 5 3 2	♣ K 9	♣ K 2	♣ Q 5

7	8	9	10*	11	12
♠ K J 3	♠ Q 10 3 2	♠ J	♠ A Q 4 3	♠ 7 6 4 2	♠ 7 3 2
♥ K Q J 9	♥ 8 5 4	♥ K Q J 10 5 3	♥ A K 7	♥ 10 7	♥ Q J 10 9 5
♦ 8 7 5 2	♦ 9 6 3	♦ A 9 8 2	♦ K Q 10 7 2	♦ A J 10 8	♦ K 7 6
♣ J 10	♣ A 6 5	♣ 9 3	♣ 9	♣ A 10 9	♣ 6 2

13	14*	15	16	17	18*
♠ 9 5 2	♠ 976432	♠ 10 8 6 3 2	♠ K 5 2	♠ 7 5 4	♠ 8 6 4 3
♥ - - -	♥ A K Q	♥ J 8 6 5	♥ Q J 7	♥ 9 5 4 2	♥ 8 7
♦ 1087654	♦ K Q	♦ 9 4	♦ A K Q	♦ K Q 10 9	♦ 5 4 3 2
♣ 10 5 4 3	♣ Q 9	♣ 7 5	♣ J 9 4 2	♣ 10 3	♣ 5 4 3

19	20	21	22*	23	24
♠ 9 7 4 2	♠ A K Q 5 4 3 2	♠ A K 7	♠ K Q 10	♠ 9 6 5 4 3	♠ A J 7 3
♥ K 10 7	♥ A K	♥ A 8 2	♥ Q J 8	♥ A 8	♥ K Q
♦ 9 6 5	♦ A J	♦ A Q 3	♦ 8 4	♦ K 2	♦ 8 7 3
♣ A K Q	♣ J 8	♣ K Q 5 4	♣ K 9 7 6 2	♣ 9 6 5 4	♣ J 10 8 4

25	26*	27	28	29	30*
♠ 10	♠ 4 2	♠ A Q 7 6 2	♠ A 9 5	♠ 6 5 4 3	♠ Q 8 4 2
♥ K Q J 8 3	♥ Q 4	♥ K 5 4 3 2	♥ K 10 5 4	♥ 9 5	♥ Q J 10 7
♦ A J 5	♦ 6 3	♦ 7	♦ A 6	♦ A	♦ Q 9 8
♣ 6 5 4 2	♣ K Q J 8 7 6 3	♣ 10 2	♣ A K Q J	♣ A Q J 8 6 3	♣ K 9

31	32	33	34*	35	36
♠ A K J 9 8 4	♠ Q 6	♠ A 2	♠ J 5 4 3	♠ 10 9 7 4 2	♠ 5
♥ K	♥ J	♥ 9 8 7 3 2	♥ A Q 2	♥ 10 8 6	♥ A Q J 10
♦ K 7 5	♦ Q J 10 9 6 4	♦ K 3	♦ K Q J 8 4	♦ A 10 3	♦ A Q 5 2
♣ 10 5 3	♣ A Q 8 7	♣ Q 10 6 2	♣ Q	♣ 9 5	♣ K 8 7 2

Play Hands for SOUTH (* = dealer)

1	2	3*	4	5	6
♠ K 8	♠ K 5 4	♠ 9 8 6	♠ K Q	♠ K J 4	♠ A 6
♥ A 7 6	♥ A J 10 9 8 7	♥ K 8 7 5	♥ J 4 3	♥ A K 7 2	♥ K Q J 9 7
♦ K 4 3 2	♦ Q 10 8 7	♦ A 9 7	♦ A 10 6 5 3	♦ A 8 5	♦ 9 8 3
♣ A 9 7 3	♣ - - -	♣ 9 7 4	♣ Q J 4	♣ J 6 3	♣ 9 7 2

7*	8	9	10	11*	12
♠ 7 6 4	♠ 9 6 5	♠ 7 6 5 4	♠ 7 5 2	♠ A K 9	♠ K Q J 10 6
♥ A 8	♥ K J 10 2	♥ 9 7 2	♥ Q J 10 9 3	♥ A K 8 6 4 3	♥ A 7 3
♦ K J 10 4	♦ K J 10 7	♦ J 5 4	♦ A 6	♦ 7 6	♦ 5 4
♣ 8 4 3 2	♣ Q 3	♣ A K Q	♣ A Q 5	♣ Q 5	♣ J 9 8

13	14	15*	16	17	18
♠ Q J	♠ Q 10 8	♠ K	♠ Q 9 8 6	♠ 8 6 2	♠ Q J 9
♥ 7 6 5 4 3	♥ 9 6	♥ A 10 7 3	♥ A 5	♥ Q J 8 7 6 3	♥ A 6 4
♦ Q J 3 2	♦ 10 8 6 2	♦ J 6 3	♦ 8 6 3	♦ 7	♦ Q 10 7
♣ A K	♣ A K 10 5	♣ A J 10 9 3	♣ Q 10 7 5	♣ 8 6 5	♣ J 10 9 6

19*	20	21	22	23*	24
♠ K Q 8 6	♠ J 10 9	♠ 10 8 3	♠ A 2	♠ 7	♠ - - -
♥ A Q J	♥ 8 6	♥ 7 5	♥ A K 6 4	♥ 10 9 7 5 3 2	♥ 7 6 5 4 3 2
♦ A K Q	♦ K 5	♦ J 10 9 8	♦ K Q J 7 6 5	♦ 6 3	♦ J 6 2
♣ J 4 2	♣ A K 6 5 4 3	♣ A 9 7 6	♣ 8	♣ A K J 3	♣ A 7 3 2

25	26	27*	28	29	30
♠ 4 2	♠ J 8 5	♠ 8	♠ K Q J 8	♠ Q J 7 2	♠ A 7
♥ A 7	♥ J 9 2	♥ 10 7	♥ Q J	♥ A Q J 10 7	♥ A 8 6 5 4 3
♦ 9 7 6 4 3 2	♦ Q 7 5 4 2	♦ A Q J 8 6 5 4 3 2	♦ 8 7 5 4	♦ J 4	♦ A K
♣ Q J 10	♣ A 10	♣ 5	♣ 9 5 2	♣ 9 4	♣ 10 6 3

31*	32	33	34	35*	36
♠ 7 6	♠ J 10 9	♠ 9	♠ A K 10 6	♠ 6 3	♠ 8 6 4
♥ Q J 10 7 6	♥ K Q 6 3	♥ A J 10	♥ 9 8 3	♥ A J 4 2	♥ 9 5
♦ A Q 6 3	♦ 8 2	♦ Q 8 7 2	♦ 5 2	♦ 9 8 6 4	♦ 10 7 6 3
♣ A 2	♣ 6 5 3 2	♣ A K 9 8 7	♣ A K 7 4	♣ 10 7 6	♣ 9 6 4 3

Play Hands for WEST (* = dealer)

1	2	3	4*	5	6
♠ 6 5	♠ 8 7 6	♠ Q J	♠ A 6 4	♠ 7 6	♠ Q J 2
♥ KQJ1082	♥ K 6	♥ 6 3 2	♥ 10 9 8 5	♥ J 10 9	♥ 8 6 5
♦ A 8	♦ 9 4 3	♦ J 8 5 2	♦ 8 4	♦ 10 6 3	♦ 7 6 4
♣ J 8 5	♣ AKQJ2	♣ A K Q J	♣ A 10 7 5	♣ A Q 9 7 4	♣ A K J 6

7	8*	9	10	11	12*
♠ A 10 5 2	♠ A K J	♠ 10 2	♠ K J 9 8	♠ Q J 10 8	♠ A 9 8
♥ 10 3 2	♥ A 7 3	♥ 4	♥ 6 5 4	♥ Q J 5	♥ K 4 2
♦ 9 6 3	♦ A 5 4 2	♦ K 10 7 6	♦ J 5	♦ 5 4 2	♦ Q J 8
♣ 9 7 5	♣ 10 8 7	♣ 876542	♣ J 8 7 3	♣ K 6 3	♣ A K Q 3

13	14	15	16*	17	18
♠ A K 8 6 3	♠ A K J 5	♠ Q J 4	♠ AJ10743	♠ K 10 9	♠ A K 7 5 2
♥ J 9 8 2	♥ J 7 3 2	♥ 9	♥ K 8 4	♥ 10	♥ K Q
♦ A 9	♦ J 9 4	♦ AKQ107	♦ J 10	♦ 8 6 5 3	♦ A K J 6
♣ Q 9	♣ J 6	♣ 8 6 4 2	♣ 6 3	♣ A K 7 4 2	♣ K Q

19	20*	21	22	23	24*
♠ J 10 5 3	♠ 7 6	♠ Q J 4	♠ 987543	♠ 10 8	♠ K86542
♥ 9 4	♥ 10 5 3 2	♥ K Q 6	♥ 10	♥ 6	♥ A
♦ J 10 8	♦ 9 8 6 3	♦ K 7 4	♦ 10 9 3	♦ 1098754	♦ A K 5 4
♣ 10 9 8 6	♣ Q 10 7	♣ J 8 3 2	♣ 10 4 3	♣ Q 10 8 7	♣ K Q

25	26	27	28*	29	30
♠ J 8 3	♠ A 10 9 3	♠ K109543	♠ 7	♠ 10 9 8	♠ KJ1093
♥ 109654	♥ A 6 5	♥ 9 8 6	♥ A987632	♥ 4 3	♥ K 9
♦ K Q 10	♦ A K 10	♦ - - -	♦ Q J 10	♦ 8 7 6 5 2	♦ 10 5 2
♣ A K	♣ 9 5 4	♣ K Q J 4	♣ 4 3	♣ K 7 2	♣ A Q 8

31	32*	33	34	35	36*
♠ Q 10 3	♠ 875432	♠ K Q 6 5	♠ Q 9 7 2	♠ 8 5	♠ A 9 3 2
♥ 8 5 4	♥ 7 4	♥ K Q 5 4	♥ 7	♥ Q 9	♥ 7 4 3
♦ J 10 9 4	♦ A 7 5	♦ A J 6 4	♦ 10 9 7 3	♦ Q J 7 5 2	♦ K J 8
♣ K Q 7	♣ 9 4	♣ 4	♣ 10 8 5 3	♣ A K J 8	♣ Q J 5

WHAT DO YOUR PARTNER'S RESPONSES MEAN?

You Partner	Meaning of Your Partner's Bid	Page
1NT : 2C	Stayman Convention, asking for opener's majors.	127
1NT : 2D / 2H / 2S	Weakness rescue from 1NT. Opener should pass.	44
1NT : 2NT	Inviting game. Opener bids 3NT if not minimum.	34, 35
1NT : 3-any-suit	Forcing to game. 5-card suit. Opener raises with 3.	56
1NT : 3NT	Sign-off in game. Opener must pass.	34
1NT : 4H or 4S	Sign-off. 6-card or longer suit. Opener must pass.	56
1C : 1D / 1H / 1S	One-over-one response. 6 or more points. Forcing.	39, 54
1C : 2D / 2H / 2S	Jump-shift. 19+ points. Game force. Suggests slam.	55, 56
1C : 3D / 3H / 3S	Pre-emptive, weak hand, 6 tricks, 7- or 8-card suit.	88–89
1C : 4H or 4S	Pre-emptive, weak hand, 7 tricks, 7- or 8-card suit.	88–89
1C / 1D : 2C / 2D	Weak raise. No major. Opener passes below 16 pts.	38
1C / 1D : 3C / 3D	Strong raise but still denies a major suit.	54–55
1C / 1D : 1NT	Weak response. Denies a major. Used as last resort.	40, 60
1C / 1D : 2NT	Strong balanced hand. Denies a major suit.	55
1C / 1D : 3NT	Stronger balanced hand. Denies a major suit.	55
1D : 1H / 1S	4-card or longer suit. 6 or more points. Forcing.	39, 54
1D : 2C	4-card or longer suit. 10 or more points. Forcing.	54–55
1D : 2H / 2S / 3C	Jump-shift. 19+ points. Game force. Suggests slam.	55, 56
1D : 3H / 3S	Pre-emptive, weak hand, 6 tricks, 7- or 8-card suit.	88–89
1D : 4H or 4S	Pre-emptive, weak hand, 7 tricks, 7- or 8-card suit.	88–89
1H / 1S : 2H / 2S	Weak raise. Opener passes below 16 points.	38
1H / 1S : 3H / 3S	Strong raise with 4-card or better support.	54–55
1H / 1S : 4H / 4S	Pre-emptive raise, usually 6–10 HCP unbalanced.	44
1H / 1S : 1NT	Weak response. 1 ♥: 1NT denies 4 spades.	40–41
1H / 1S : 2NT	Strong balanced hand. Denies the other major.	55
1H / 1S : 3NT	Stronger balanced hand. Denies the other major.	55
1H : 1S	Four or more spades, 6 or more points. Forcing.	41
1H / 1S : 2C / 2D	4-card or longer suit, 10 or more points. Forcing.	54–55
1S : 2H	*Five* or more hearts, 10 or more points. Forcing.	57
1S : 3H	Jump shift. 19+ points. Game force. Suggests slam.	55–56
1S : 4H	Pre-emptive, weak hand, 7 tricks, 7- or 8-card suit.	89
1H / 1S : 3C / 3D	Jump shift. 19+ points. Game force. Suggests slam.	55–56
Any suit : 4NT	Blackwood Convention, asking for aces.	82
1NT : 4NT	Invites 6NT. Opener passes if absolutely minimum.	83
2NT : 4NT	Invites 6NT. Opener passes if absolutely minimum.	83
3NT : 4NT	Invites 6NT. Opener passes if absolutely minimum.	83
2NT : 3C	Stayman. (For Baron Convention, see page 149.)	128
2NT : 3D / 3H / 3S	5-card suit. Forcing to game. Opener raises with 3.	69
2NT : 4H or 4S	Sign off. 6-card or longer suit. Opener must pass.	69

Rubber Bridge Scoring Table

Points Towards Game Under the Line:

No-trumps—	First trick	40
	Subsequent tricks	30
Spades or Hearts (major suits)		30
Diamonds or Clubs (minor suits)		20

Final contract doubled and made: Double the above values
Final contract redoubled and made: Above values x 4

Bonus Points Above the Line:

OVERTRICKS		*Not vulnerable*	*Vulnerable*
For each	Not doubled	Trick value	Trick value
overtrick	Doubled	100	200
	Redoubled	200	400

SLAMS AND BIDS MADE	*Not vulnerable*	*Vulnerable*
Small slam	500	750
Grand slam	1000	1500

For Defeating a Contract:

Not doubled, each undertrick: 50 not vulnerable, 100 if vulnerable
Doubled, not vulnerable: 1st undertrick 100, 2nd and 3rd 200, others 300
Doubled and vulnerable: 1st undertrick 200, all others 300
Redoubled: All undertricks score at twice the doubled rate above

For Making a Doubled Contract: **50**
For Making a Redoubled Contract: **100**

For Honors:

Four trump honors in one hand	100
Five trump honors in one hand	150
Four aces in one hand if the contract is no-trumps	150

(Either side can score honors, which are claimed at the end of play.)

For Winning the Rubber:

For winning by two games to nil 700

For winning by two games to one..500

For one game if the rubber is unfinished 300

For partscore if rubber is unfinished 50

(If scoring game by game: Game 1: 350; Game 2: 350; Game 3: 500.)

Duplicate Score:

Points for honors or winning the rubber do not apply. For making a partscore, add 50 to the tricks score. For making a game, add 300 if not vulnerable, or 500 if vulnerable. All other scoring is as above.

Notes

Notes

Notes

Notes

Notes